D1241890

MEDIA PLANNING:

A Practical Guide

MEDIA PLANNING:

A Practical Guide

Jim Surmanek

CRAIN BOOKS, an imprint of
NTC NATIONAL TEXTBOOK COMPANY • Lincolnwood, Illinois U.S.A.

Published by Crain Books, an imprint of National
Textbook Company, 4255 West Touhy Avenue,
Lincolnwood, Illinois 60646-1975

Library of Congress Number: 85-62136
International Standard Book Number: 0-8442-3046-4

Manufactured in the United States of America.

5 6 7 8 9 0 ML 9 8 7 6 5 4 3 2 1

To Paula.

Contents

Foreword

The media professional in the advertising agency has come a long way since the days when I started in the business—in the early 1950s.

In those days, media was a relatively simple, mundane part of an agency's operations. *Life, Look, Saturday Evening Post*, and some important radio programs were the core of most major advertisers' plans.

This is in no way a reflection on the quality of the media professional. There simply weren't that many choices available. All that has changed, not just a little, but radically.

It doesn't take a media expert to realize how different things are today. Just look around. The *Saturday Evening Post* and *Look* are memories. *Life* has been reincarnated, but only as one of a myriad of special interest magazines overflowing our magazine racks.

Television, which has dominated the advertising scene (and our lives as well), is undergoing a major facelift, challenged by the new boys in town—cable, videocassettes, satellites, and computers.

The menu of choices for the advertisers and the consumer is bewildering. A typical *TV Guide* today resembles a telephone book, with two pages for *each hour* of listings instead of two pages for *each evening* just ten years ago. Coping with and capitalizing on these changes is one of the major tasks facing the advertising business today. And the finger is pointing squarely at the media expert to take a leadership role in meeting this challenge.

Unquestionably, the media professional is in the catbird seat. Not only has the responsibility of these experts expanded enormously, but the impact of the decisions they make has greater leverage than ever before . . . on the advertising, the marketing plan, and the management of the advertising investment.

This spotlight on media has also required non-media specialists to upgrade their own skills in understanding the media planning process. No advertiser practitioner today, regardless of specialty, can do justice to the craft without a working knowledge of and sensitivity to the transformations taking place in the media world.

Jim Surmanek's book on media planning couldn't be more timely. But there is more to this book than just good timing: it is a practitioner's book written by someone who has performed media planning in the *real world* and done it brilliantly.

It is a wonderfully clear and concise overview of the fundamentals of media planning as done on the firing line for real clients, in tough new business presentations, as taught by major agencies to the new people entering the business. Surmanek doesn't just define and explain the tools of the trade; he helps you understand how to apply them. The chapters on "How to Present Media," "Media Creativity," and "Media Management" are good illustrations of taking the reader beyond the mechanics.

Given the increased prominence of media planning in the advertising process, any book on the subject would be extraordinarily useful. How fortunate that this is more than just any book . . . it is a very good book.

—*Jules Fine*

Preface

Advertising media are dynamic and ever changing. The entire spectrum of media outlets changes almost daily. There are constantly new magazines being published, new radio stations, and old radio stations that change their formats, new television programs, new ways to reach people within television. Media vehicles tend to follow people's lifestyle shifts in order to address consumers' needs effectively. To the extent that people change, so do the media.

Additionally, the marketplace for buying and selling advertising time and space also changes dramatically. The cost of advertising in television and radio fluctuates up and down depending on supply and demand. Commercial time in broadcast media is both limited and perishable. If demand is high, the sellers increase their advertising rates. But unsold inventory cannot be saved and advertising costs can decrease if demand is low.

No book, no article, is current. By the time most books are published, they are somewhat outdated. The basic concept of what is being stated generally holds true; the specifics, though, will always change.

As of this writing, we have a body of knowledge to guide us in our media decisions. Published research is available. And a myriad of additional research is in the field, or about to be published, or on the media planner's desk awaiting sanction.

As time goes on, more knowledge will be accumulated. It is the writer's hope that this increased storehouse will further guide advertisers and advertising media planners to select the right medium, at the right price and at the right time.

—J.S.

Introduction

Much has been written in books, pamphlets and trade periodicals by a host of advertising experts about advertising media. Consuming that vast storehouse of literature would be extremely beneficial to anyone desiring to understand the complexities and dynamics of media planning.

This book is not meant to replace that library. Its purpose is rather to highlight the basic dynamics of media planning—from the formulation of advertising objectives to the understanding of intricate definitions; from understanding the relationship of one medium to another to comprehending the relationship between various analytical devices used to evaluate media.

The book is divided into two parts:

Part I systematically deals with the definitions and dynamics of various media forms.

Part II broadly outlines the ingredients used in formulating a media plan and discusses ancillary topics with which the media planner should be familiar in order to plan effective advertising efforts.

The Glossary/Index is a handy reference defining the most common terms used in media planning, as well as referring the reader to the specific page where that term is discussed.

If the reader is relatively new to advertising media planning, or has had little involvement with media, he or she might best start at the beginning of the book (with basic definitions). If the reader is familiar with the many terms used in media planning, he or she would be better served by starting with Part II, referring to the Glossary/Index when encountering an unfamiliar term.

PART I
DEFINITIONS AND DYNAMICS

Overview

Different media forms are used for different purposes. Generally no one specific medium can accomplish all the objectives of a media plan. More often than not, several media offer benefits that should be taken advantage of if the advertising budget and copy flexibility permit. The media planner and media buyer must have intimate knowledge of the dynamics of each medium to devise the proper media solution and purchase media in the most efficient and effective way.

The more popular mass media are compared on several general bases in Table 1. We should keep in mind that the comparisons are *general* and based on *average* use of each medium. When used for different purposes, each medium can produce different results.

The terms in the chart are media jargon, part of a specialized language we have developed to describe the dynamics we deal with in advertising media planning. These terms and others are defined and discussed in this section. They are not presented in any order. All are equally important and should be thoroughly understood by the media professional and by those indirectly involved in media decisions. Inter-related terms, however, are presented in sequential order to help the reader better understand media dynamics. For example, "Rating," "HUT" and "Share," though distinctly different terms, tend to be used in combination in media analysis.

Table 1. Characteristics of major media forms.

	Broadcast TV	Cable TV	Radio	Magazines
Unit used for comparison purposes	:30	:30	:60	4-color page
Cost-per-thousand	Average	Low	Low	Average
Audience selectivity	Fair	Good	Good	Excellent
Reach potential	95%	45%	60%	70%
Speed of audience accumulation	Excellent	Good	Good	Poor
Geographic flexibility	Excellent	Poor	Excellent	Fair
Timing flexibility for purchase	Good	Good	Good	Poor

	News-papers	Supple-ments	Outdoor	Transit
Unit used for comparison purposes	Page	4-color page	#100	#100
Cost-per-thousand	High	High	Low	Low
Audience selectivity	Fair	Fair	Poor	Poor
Reach potential	85%	75%	95%	95%
Speed of audience accumulation	Excellent	Excellent	Fair	Fair
Geographic flexibility	Excellent	Excellent	Excellent	Good
Timing flexibility for purchase	Excellent	Fair	Poor	Fair

Rating

A rating is the percentage of individuals (or homes) tuned to a particular television or radio program.

Let us assume a total television household population (those owning a TV set) of five homes. As shown in the example, two of the five television homes are viewing Program A. Program A's rating is therefore 40, or two divided by five (the percent sign is dropped). Program B has a rating of 20, as does Program C, because one of the five homes owning a TV set is viewing each of these programs.

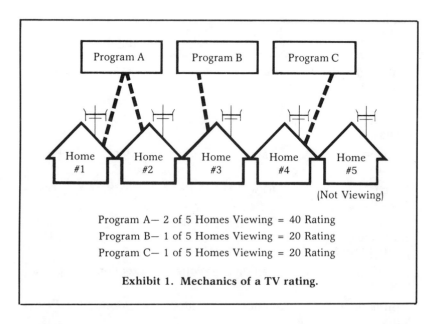

Program A— 2 of 5 Homes Viewing = 40 Rating
Program B— 1 of 5 Homes Viewing = 20 Rating
Program C— 1 of 5 Homes Viewing = 20 Rating

Exhibit 1. Mechanics of a TV rating.

The same dynamics apply to calculating a rating for people (as opposed to homes). If two people live in each of these five homes, the total population against which a rating is devised is ten. As shown in the following chart, one person in Home #1 is viewing Program A while the other person is not viewing. Both people in Home #2 are viewing program B, and so on for the remaining homes. In total, one person is viewing Program A, producing a rating of 10 (one divided into the total TV population of ten). Program B has a 30 rating, and Program C a 20 rating.

Table 2. Number of People Viewing.

	Program A	Program B	Program C	Not Viewing	Total
Home #1	1	—	—	1	2
Home #2	—	2	—	—	2
Home #3	—	1	—	1	2
Home #4	—	—	2	—	2
Home #5	—	—	—	2	2
Total	1	3	2	4	10
Rating	10	30	20		

Rating is the most important broadcast term. Advertisers and agencies use ratings to buy television and radio programs, to determine how many people will be reached with their advertising messages and to calculate how often they will be exposed to these messages.

Broadcasters, such as the three television networks, use ratings to assess a program's popularity. If the rating for a program is high, the program will probably continue to be kept on-air. Conversely, if the rating is low, the program would, more often than not, be cancelled.

Broadcasters also use ratings as one criterion for establishing prices for commercials. Generally, the higher rated programs command higher prices.

Top advertising agencies spend more money for rating information from various research syndicators than for any other media research tool. And each individual television network spends more for rating information than any single agency.

Homes Using TV (HUT)

HUT is the percentage of homes using television at a given time of the day.

As shown, the first two homes are viewing Program A; the next home, Program B; and the next, Program C. The fifth home is not using television at this time. Of the five TV homes, four are viewing. Expressed as a percentage, the HUT at this time is 80 percent.

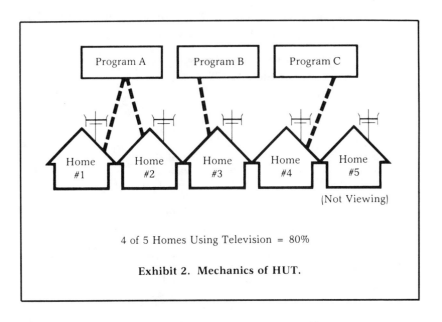

4 of 5 Homes Using Television = 80%

Exhibit 2. Mechanics of HUT.

In this example, we use television *homes*. The same concept applies to *People* Using Television (PUT), and *People* Using Radio. The difference in the terms derives from the population base to which we refer.

Hypothetically, although 80 percent of *homes* are using television in the example shown, the percentage of total *people* using television could be less. If we assume there are two persons in every home, and only one is viewing television, the PUT would be 40 percent—four people viewing divided by a population base of ten people.

In all cases, the percentage refers to the available universe with a TV set or radio set *in their home*, rather than to the total population.

HUT levels vary by season, by time of day, by geographic area and by market. The variations reflect work habits and life style. Usage levels are lower in the morning when people are going to work. They are higher at night when people are home, but get lower as the evening wears on and people go to sleep. They are lower in warmer weather when people tend to stay outdoors more, and higher in colder weather.

The following table demonstrates typical variations in HUT levels according to Eastern Standard Time. Interestingly, be-

Table 3. HUT variations.

By Season (8–11 p.m. EST)		By Time of Day	
Jan–Mar	64%	8–8:30 p.m.	56%
Apr–Jun	53%	8:30–9	58%
Jul–Sep	48%	9–9:30	59%
Oct–Dec	61%	9:30–10	59%
Annual average	57%	10–10:30	57%
		10:30–11	53%
		Average 8–11 p.m.	57%
By Geography (11 p.m.–1 a.m. EST)		By Market (11 p.m.–1 a.m. EST)	
Northeast	29%	New York	30%
Central	36%	Portland, Me.	11%
South	25%	Chicago	42%
West	22%	Des Moines	33%
National average	29%	Miami	21%
		Columbus, Ga.	18%
		Los Angeles	26%
		Reno	13%

Source: A. C. Nielsen

cause the Central Region receives primetime television fare one hour earlier than the Eastern or Western regions, HUT levels in the Central area tend to be higher than average.

The usage level of television and radio complement each other: Radio listening is at its highest level when TV is at its lowest, and vice versa.

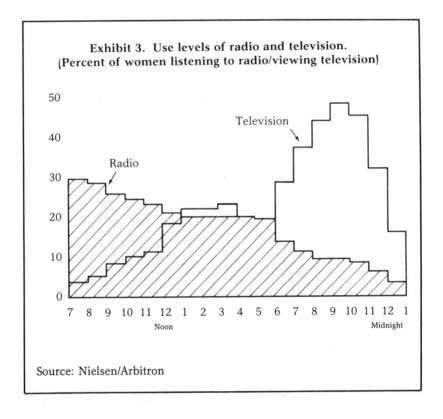

Exhibit 3. Use levels of radio and television.
(Percent of women listening to radio/viewing television)

Source: Nielsen/Arbitron

The reader should keep in mind that although the dynamics of the media terms are the same regardless of the population base referred to (homes, or men, or women, etc.), the absolute numbers can vary substantially. The above chart, for example, shows that approximately 48 percent of women view television between 9:00 and 10:00 p.m. This compares to Table 3, which shows a HUT level of 59. This difference is explained by the fact that other viewing population segments (men, for example) are causing additional *homes* to be counted as viewing households.

Let us assume there are five TV homes, each with four people (one man, one woman, one teenager, one child). As shown in the following table, two people are viewing in Home #1, two in Home #2 and one each in Homes #3 and #4. No one is viewing in Home #5. In total, four of the five homes are viewing: an 80 *HUT*. The *PUT* levels, however, are lower and vary by population segment: 20 for men, 40 for women, 20 for teens, 40 for children and 30 for all people on average.

Table 4. Number of Viewers.					
	Men	Women	Teens	Children	Total
Home #1	1	1	—	—	2
Home #2	—	1	—	1	2
Home #3	—	—	1	—	1
Home #4	—	—	—	1	1
Home #5	—	—	—	—	—
Total	1	2	1	2	6
Pop. Base	5	5	5	5	20
PUT	20	40	20	40	30

Share

Share is the *percentage of HUT* tuned to a particular program.

In business, "market share" is used as a benchmark to express what percentage of the total industry sales dollars a company has for itself. "Share" in television is used in a similar fashion. It states what percentage a program, or station, has of the total viewing/listening audience.

Keep in mind that share is not projected to the total homes owning a TV set, but only to those homes *viewing* at a particular time.

In the following exhibit, Program A is viewed by two of the five TV homes available, but only four TV homes are viewing. Program A is therefore being viewed by 50 percent of the viewing audience and has a 50 share.

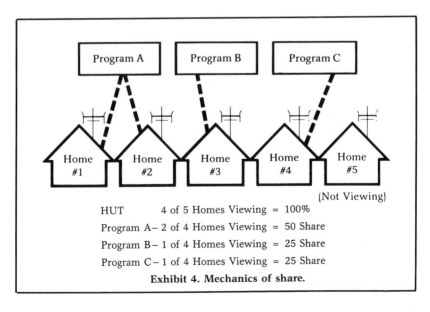

HUT	4 of 5 Homes Viewing = 100%
Program A– 2 of 4 Homes Viewing = 50 Share
Program B– 1 of 4 Homes Viewing = 25 Share
Program C– 1 of 4 Homes Viewing = 25 Share

Exhibit 4. Mechanics of share.

The share of a program in daytime might be the same as a program at nighttime, but because so many more homes are viewing TV at night than in the day, the ratings of the programs are quite different—the ones at night being higher.

Rating/HUT/Share

These three terms are interrelated. By knowing any two, we can calculate the third. As a formula, rating, share and HUT can be expressed as follows:

HUT × Share = Rating

Tying the three terms together in the chart below, we see:

- 80 percent of the homes owning a TV set are viewing—80 percent HUT.
- Program A is viewed by two of the five homes—40 rating.
- Of the four TV homes viewing, two are viewing Program A—50 percent share.

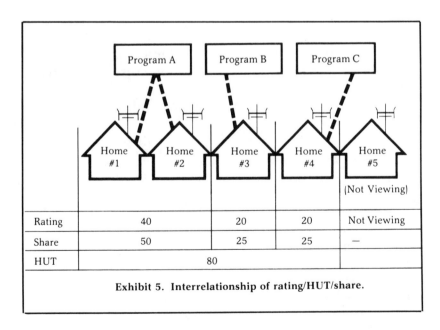

	Program A	Program B	Program C	
Rating	40	20	20	Not Viewing
Share	50	25	25	—
HUT	80			

Exhibit 5. Interrelationship of rating/HUT/share.

Table 5. Rating, HUT, and Share.

Program	Day–Time	Rating			
		Women	Men	Teens	Child.
A Team	Tu 8–9PM	15.7	15.7	19.3	19.3
Murder, She Wrote	Su 8:30–9:30PM	16.4	13.0	8.2	7.3
Kate & Allie	Mo 9–9:30PM	16.8	8.1	11.9	6.5
General Hospital	M–F 3–4PM	7.4	2.6	4.2	2.4
Silver Spoons	Su 7–7:30PM	5.6	5.8	8.8	15.5

Program	Day–Time	Household		
		Rating	Share	HUT
A Team	Tu 8–9PM	22.2	33	67
Murder, She Wrote	Su 8:30–9:30PM	22.2	32	69
Kate & Allie	Mo 9–9:30PM	19.5	28	70
General Hospital	M–F 3–4PM	8.7	28	31
Silver Spoons	Su 7–7:30PM	8.8	14	63

Source: A.C. Nielsen

Table 5 is designed to give the reader a sense of rating, HUT and share as usually shown in syndicated research sources; to reinforce how the three terms are interrelated; and to demonstrate why all three terms are independently important in any media analysis.

Studying this information the reader will note the following:

- *A Team* and *Murder, She Wrote* had the same household rating, about the same share, and aired in time periods with similar HUT levels.
- Although women and men ratings can be considered similar between the two programs, the ratings among teens and children are quite different.
- The ratings among "people" are always less than the ratings for "homes."
- *Kate & Allie* and *General Hospital* have the same "share," but the ratings vary substantially because the HUT levels vary widely during their respective time periods.

- *General Hospital* and *Silver Spoons* have the same house-hold rating but distinctly different "shares."

ESTIMATING A RATING

We can estimate, with some degree of accuracy, the share a program might receive. Just *some* of the variables considered are: time period (when the show will air); the competition the show will have on the other stations (will the new program be opposite a top-rated program or a weak program?); programs preceding and following the new program (a strong lead-in program is sometimes advantageous if we assume viewers will not change channels too readily); the type of program (will it be a documentary or a situation comedy?); the history of similar types of programs (were they hits or misses?). We also study the script, screen the pilot when available, and know the producer, director and cast to determine if their talents have produced successes in the past.

If a new program is to air on Tuesdays between 9 and 9:30 p.m., we know that about 66 percent of the homes will be viewing TV. If we estimate the share of audience the program might receive—based on all of the above variables—we can estimate the rating of the program.

HUT	66%
Share	× 35%
Rating	23.1

The key word is *estimate*. It is a judgment calculated from imperfect data. Although it is based on extensive analysis of past performance, it is, nevertheless, only an estimate of what the media professional believes *will* happen.

A corollary to Murphy's Law might be "If anything can vary it will." As we have seen, HUT varies by time of day and by season. Share varies for all the reasons previously stated. These differences result in rating variations—from airing to airing and from moment to moment while the program is on air. Table 6 shows the rating received by *A Team* for two consecutive airings and for each quarter hour within each airing.

Even if the media planner or buyer had accurately estimated *A Team*'s average rating, the real audience could have varied substantially: from a high rating of 24.3 to a low of 18.4.

Time	Table 6. "A Team" Household Ratings.		
	Week I	Week II	Average
8:00–8:15	20.2	18.4	19.3
8:15–8:30	22.8	19.8	21.3
8:30–8:45	24.3	23.6	24.0
8:45–9:00	24.3	23.6	24.0
Average	22.9	21.4	22.2

Source: A.C. Nielsen

Gross Rating Points (GRPs)

Gross Rating Points are the sum of the ratings delivered by a given list of media vehicles. Like ratings, GRPs are a percentage.

GRPs offer a description of total audience delivery without regard to duplication or repeat exposure to the media vehicles, thus the word *gross*. Individuals, or homes, are counted as many times as they are exposed to the advertising.

To calculate GRPs, we multiply the rating of each announcement (or magazine insertion, etc.) by the number of times each announcement runs. If a program with a 20 rating is used twice, total GRPs are 40 (20 × 2). The schedule shown, composed of 13 announcements across four programs, delivers 200 GRPs.

Table 7. Calculating gross rating points.

	Average Household Rating	Announcements in Schedule	GRPs
Program A	20	2	40
Program B	15	4	60
Program C	25	2	50
Program D	10	5	50
		13	200

If a 20 rated program is seen by 20 percent of the households with a TV set, then two announcements scheduled in this program will be seen by the *equivalent* of 40 percent of households. The 13-announcement schedule shown above, with 200

GRPs, will therefore be seen once by the *equivalent* of 200 percent of the population.

GRPs are one way to express total gross audience delivery. Impressions, discussed on the next page, represent another way to express gross delivery.

Impressions

Impressions are the sum of all advertising exposures. Impressions are the same as GRPs, but are expressed in terms of *numbers* of individuals (or homes) rather than as a percentage.

Impressions can be calculated in one of two ways:

- Multiply the GRPs delivered to a given population group by the number of people in the population group.
- Add the audience delivered (number) for each announcement (or magazine insertion, etc.) in a schedule.

Table 8. Calculating impressions.

	Households (000)	Announcements in Schedule	Impressions (000)
Program A	17,000	2	34,000
Program B	12,750	4	51,000
Program C	21,250	2	42,500
Program D	8,500	5	42,500
Total		13	170,000

Assumed population base: 85 million homes

Let us assume the 13-announcement schedule shown before, which delivers 200 household GRPs, is broadcast to all TV homes in the United States. Let us further assume, for simplicity's sake, that there are 85 million homes with TV sets in the U.S. Using the first method for calculating impressions, we would multiply the 200 GRPs (200 percent) by 85 million homes, yielding a product of 170 million homes, or impressions.

Likewise, the households reached by each program, multiplied by the number of announcements in that program, will also yield 170 million impressions.

Impressions, like GRPs, indicate the *gross* delivery without regard to multiple exposure to the same persons. The 13-announcement schedule will be seen by the *equivalent* of 140 million homes, but not by 140 million *different* homes.

As will be discussed later, GRPs and Impressions are useful tools for analyzing and buying media, but neither indicates how many *different* people will be exposed to the media forms nor how many *times* they will be exposed. Enter two more terms: Reach and Frequency.

Reach

Reach is the number of *different* individuals (or homes) exposed to a media schedule within a given period of time, generally expressed as a percentage.

Exhibit 6 shows a population of 100 TV homes—each box equivalent to one home. Let us assume that you have purchased a schedule of one commercial in each of four different

Exhibit 6. Calculating TV reach. 100 TV HOMES									
A	A	A	A	A	B	B	B	C	C
C	C	D	D	D	D	D	AB	AB	AC
AC	AD	AD	BC	BC	BD	BD	BD	ABC	ABC
BCD	BCD	BCD	ACD	ACD	ABDC	ABDC	ABDC	ABDC	ABDC

TV programs (A, B, C and D) which aired in a particular week. It is probable that many viewers saw more than one announcement. Some of the viewers of Program A might also have viewed Programs B, C, or D or any combination of these. As demonstrated, a total of 40 different homes viewed at least one of the programs. The reach of the four programs combined is therefore 40 percent (40 homes reached divided by 100 TV home population).

To tie back to *ratings*, we can see that each of the four TV programs have a 20 rating by simply counting the number of homes in which each program was viewed. Program A, for example, was viewed in 20 different homes: 20 homes divided by the 100 TV homes population yields a 20 rating. This schedule of four TV programs, each with a 20 rating, produced 80 GRPs.

To calculate *reach*, viewers are counted only once, no matter how many programs they view or how many commercials they might be exposed to. The concept of seeing more than one commercial is discussed later under the heading Frequency.

The dynamics of *reach* apply to all media forms. The only variation among media is the time frame for which reach is expressed. With broadcast media, reach is generally expressed over a four-week period. This is because the data collected by syndicated research sources is usually tabulated over a four-week period for reach calculations. With magazines or newspapers, reach is usually calculated for the total reading audience over the life of a given issue. *Reader's Digest*, for example, has an average issue life of approximately 11 to 12 weeks. That is, from the time of issuance, it will take about 11 to 12 weeks until the last person who is going to read *Reader's Digest* reads it. With out-of-home media (outdoor, transit), reach is expressed over a one-month period.

Exhibit 7 displays how many women will be reached with an advertising schedule encompassing three magazines. Again, the dynamics of reach are the same as in television but are displayed differently in this Exhibit for greater clarification.

Magazine A is read by 20 percent of all women. Some of these women also read Magazine B or Magazine C, and some read both B and C:

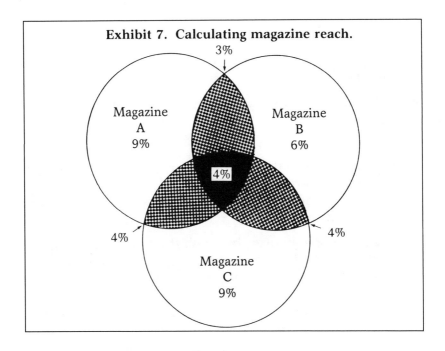

Exhibit 7. Calculating magazine reach.

9% read *only* A (exclusive audience)
3% read A and B
4% read A and C
4% read A, B and C
_____
20% read A

To determine the reach of all three magazines combined, we add the *exclusive* audiences for each to the duplicated audiences, counting the duplicated audience only once:

	Reach
A (Exclusive)	9%
B (Exclusive)	6
C (Exclusive)	9
A + B (Duplicated)	3
A + C (Duplicated)	4
B + C (Duplicated)	4
A + B + C (Duplicated)	4
Total	39%

Media Mix

Media mix refers to the use of two or more different media forms in one advertising plan.

There are a number of reasons for mixing media. Among the most common are:

- To reach people not reached with the first medium.
- To provide additional repeat exposure in a less expensive, secondary medium after optimum reach is obtained in the first medium.
- To utilize some of the intrinsic values of a medium to extend the creative effectiveness of the advertising campaign (such as music on radio or long copy in print media).
- To deliver coupons in print media when the primary media vehicle in the media plan is broadcast.
- *Synergism*, a term borrowed from chemistry, which describes an effect produced by the sum of the parts that is greater than that expected by adding together the individual components.

When two media forms are combined to increase total reach, the basic supposition is that the secondary medium provides advertising exposure opportunities beyond those offered by the first medium—the first medium, based on its usage in your media plan, has limited reach.

In Exhibit 8, 60 percent of the population are reached with a specific television schedule. This means 40 percent are *not* reached by that TV schedule. Additionally, a specific magazine schedule reaches 50 percent of people, meaning 50 percent are *not* reached with these magazines (30 percent plus 20 percent, shown in separate bars for demonstrable purposes).

An accepted statistical method for combining the reach of these two media is known as *random combination*, which

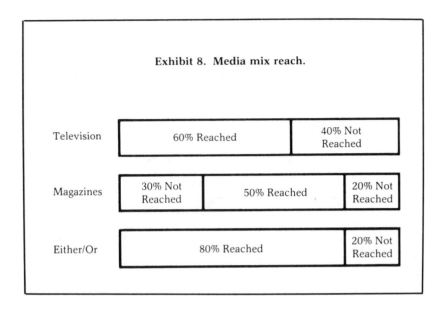

Exhibit 8. Media mix reach.

| Television | 60% Reached | 40% Not Reached |

| Magazines | 30% Not Reached | 50% Reached | 20% Not Reached |

| Either/Or | 80% Reached | 20% Not Reached |

assumes that those not reached by one medium have an opportunity to be exposed to the second medium. This opportunity increases as the proportion of those not reached by the second medium increases. Using the random technique, we can establish that 20 percent of people are not reached by either medium:

$$
\begin{array}{r}
40\% \text{ not reached in television} \\
\times\ 50\% \text{ not reached in magazines} \\
\hline
20\% \text{ not reached by either medium}
\end{array}
$$

Subtracting 20 percent from the total possible reach of 100 percent leaves 80 percent, which is the percentage the combination in this schedule supposedly *does* reach.

One last point. When combining two or more media forms, you must establish reach for all media on the same population base. You obviously cannot combine the reach of women in one medium with that of men in another medium. Nor can you combine the reach of homes equipped with cable television in a television schedule with that of total homes for a newspaper plan. In this instance, you must either calculate reach for the

Table 9. Combined reach of two media.

Reach of One Medium

Reach of Second Medium	25	30	35	40	45	50	55	60	65	70	75	80	85	90	95
25	46	47	51	55	59	62	66	70	74	77	81	85	89	92	95
30	—	51	54	58	61	65	68	72	75	79	82	86	90	93	95
35	—	—	58	61	64	67	71	74	77	80	84	87	90	93	95
40	—	—	—	64	67	70	73	76	79	82	85	88	91	94	95
45	—	—	—	—	70	72	75	78	81	83	86	89	92	94	95
50	—	—	—	—	—	75	77	80	82	85	87	90	92	95	95
55	—	—	—	—	—	—	80	82	84	86	89	91	93	95	95
60	—	—	—	—	—	—	—	84	86	88	90	92	94	95	95
65	—	—	—	—	—	—	—	—	88	89	91	93	95	95	95
70	—	—	—	—	—	—	—	—	—	91	92	94	95	95	95
75	—	—	—	—	—	—	—	—	—	—	94	95	95	95	95
80	—	—	—	—	—	—	—	—	—	—	—	95	95	95	95
85	—	—	—	—	—	—	—	—	—	—	—	—	95	95	95
90	—	—	—	—	—	—	—	—	—	—	—	—	—	95	95
95	—	—	—	—	—	—	—	—	—	—	—	—	—	—	95

television plan for total homes, or calculate reach of the newspaper plan for homes equipped with cable television.

Table 9 shows the combined reach of two media forms using the random combination technique. Referring to the previous example of a television and magazine plan, we can use this table to estimate total reach of the two media combined:

- Find the reach of the first medium on the horizontal axis—60.
- Find the reach of the second medium on the vertical axis—50.
- Read down from the 60 reach on the horizontal axis, and across from the 50 reach on the vertical axis. The point of intersection shows the combined reach—80.

If three media forms are combined, the same procedure is used: find the combined reach of the first two media, then find the reach of this combination plus the third medium:

	Reach
Medium A	60
Medium B	50
Medium A & B	80 (from table)
Medium C	35
Medium A & B & C	87 (from table)

We can also analyze media combinations in terms of the percentage who will receive only the first medium, or only the second medium, or both media.

This calculation should always be made to show exposure to each media form being used. It is often mistakingly assumed that when two media are combined, all people reached will be exposed to your advertising in *both* media. The usual effect of adding a second medium is to extend reach to those not exposed to the first medium.

To calculate "only-only-both" reach, use the following procedure:

1. Combine the two media randomly: 60% + 50% = 80%

2. Subtract the reach of medium A from the combined reach—this yields the percentage exposed to only medium B: 80% − 60% = 20%

3. Subtract the reach of medium B from the combined reach—this yields the percentage exposed to only medium A: 80% − 50% = 30%

4. Subtract the combined reach of only medium A and only medium B from the total combined reach—this yields the percentage exposed to *both* media: 80% − (20% + 30%) = 30%

If the media forms in the media plan are those shown in Exhibit 9, the planner can conclude the following:

- Television will reach 60 percent of the population against which these calculations have been made.
- Magazines will reach 50 percent.
- 80 percent will be reached by TV, or magazines, or both.
- 30 percent will be reached by TV *only*.
- 20 percent will be reached by magazines *only*.
- 30 percent will be reached by *both* TV and magazines.
- 20 percent of the population will not be reached with this advertising schedule.

Now that we have dealt with the dynamics of reach, we can turn to the other part of the equation: Frequency.

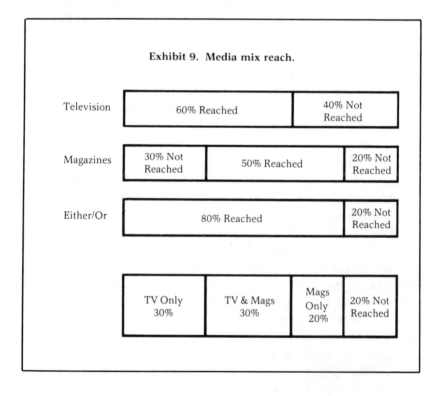

Exhibit 9. Media mix reach.

Frequency

Frequency is the *average* number of times individuals (or homes) are exposed to advertising messages.

Again, let us use the schedule as originally presented in Exhibit 6 in which one commercial was placed in each of four television programs (A, B, C, D). In Exhibit 10, a total of 40 homes viewed one or more of these four TV programs: 17 homes viewed only one program; 11 homes, two programs; seven homes, three programs; and five homes, four programs.

Exhibit 10. Frequency of advertising exposure.

A	A	A	A	A	B	B	B	C	C
C	C	D	D	D	D	D	AB	AB	AC
AC	AD	AD	BC	BC	BD	BD	BD	ABC	ABC
BCD	BCD	BCD	ACD	ACD	ABDC	ABDC	ABDC	ABDC	ABDC

If we add the number of programs each home viewed, the 40 homes in total viewed the *equivalent* of 80 programs and therefore were exposed to the *equivalent* of 80 commercials. By division (80 commercials divided by 40 homes), we establish that the average home was exposed to an average of two commercials.

Average is emphasized for two reasons: Firstly, frequency is often referred to as *Average Frequency*. Secondly, *Frequency Distribution*, an additional concept presented later, is the phenomenon of different groups of people being exposed to media forms with different levels of frequency that are produced by the same advertising schedule.

FREQUENCY IN PRINT MEDIA

The idea of frequency, like reach, is identical in all media forms. As shown in Exhibit 11, Magazines A, B and C each have "exclusive" audiences and "duplicated" audiences. For example, Magazine A is read by 20 percent of the population with 3 percent of this 20 percent also reading Magazine B, 4 percent also reading Magazine C, and 4 percent also reading both Magazines B and C. Magazines B and C have a total readership of 17 percent and 21 percent, respectively. Like Magazine A, both have exclusive and duplicated audiences, as shown in the exhibit. In total, the three magazines combined have a *gross* audience of 58 percent (20 plus 17 plus 21).

If the percent of population which reads one, two, or all three magazines is displayed as in the following table, we can see

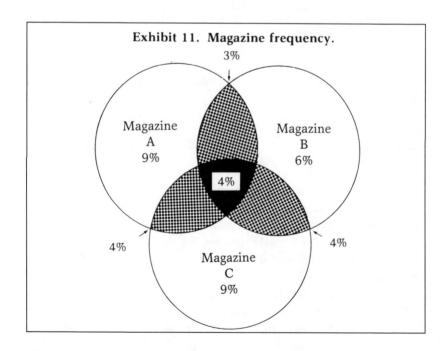

Exhibit 11. Magazine frequency.

readily how many people will be exposed to the advertisements one, two, or three times. The number of times they are exposed is the same as the frequency they will receive. In total, 39 percent of the population will be exposed *one or more* times. The average person will be exposed 1.5 times (1.5 Average Frequency). This average is obtained by dividing the *gross* audience (58 percent) by the audience who will be exposed one or more times (39 percent).

Table 10. Percent of people reached.

Magazine	1 Time	2 Times	3 Times
A	9	—	—
B	6	—	—
C	9	—	—
A + B	—	3	—
A + C	—	4	—
B + C	—	4	—
A + B + C	—	—	4
Total	24	11	4
Total—one or more times		39	
Average number of times (Average Frequency)		1.5	

Reach/Frequency/GRPs

The three terms work together. Although they are always expressed as a percentage (without the percent sign), they represent the number of people, or homes, that a media schedule will deliver. *Reach* indicates how many of the audience that you wish to deliver your advertising message(s) to will probably see/hear your advertising *one or more times*. Frequency demonstrates the *average number of times* that audience will be reached. GRPs are the product of reach and freqency and express the *gross* duplicated percentage of audience that will be reached. When the actual numbers of people are shown in gross terms, we refer to that as *Impressions*.

The following table shows a media schedule which delivers an 80 reach with a 2.0 frequency (commonly written as 80/2.0). Total GRPs are therefore 160 (80 times 2.0). Let us assume that the population base against which the R/F was calculated is 10,000,000. By multiplication we see that the 80 reach equals 8,000,000 people. These 8,000,000 will be exposed to the advertising schedule an average of two times each. Total impression delivery is therefore 16,000,000 (8,000,000 times 2.0).

	Percent	*Actual*
Reach	80.0	8,000,000
Frequency	2.0	—
GRPs	160.0	—
Impressions	—	16,000,000
Total Population	100	10,000,000

HOW REACH/FREQUENCY ARE USED

Reach and frequency are used to analyze alternative schedules to determine which produces the best results relative to the media plan's objectives.

Table 11. Reach/frequency comparisons.		
	Equal Expenditures	
	Plan I Announcements	Plan II Announcements
Prime network TV (:30)	10	5
Day network TV (:30)	20	53
	30	58
Women reached	80%	75%
Average frequency	2.8	4.2

The example shows two alternative schedules, either one of which is affordable within the budget limitations. Alternative I schedules 10 announcements in primetime network TV and 20 announcements in daytime network TV. Alternative II has 5 announcements in primetime and 53 in daytime. Both schedules cost the same.

By calculating reach and frequency, we can compare the two plans on the basis of how many people we will reach with each schedule and the number of times we will reach the average person. If reach were the only criterion, we would select Alternative I; if frequency were more important to the achievement of the media plan's objectives, Alternative II has the advantage.

HOW GRPs ARE USED

Gross Rating Points are used to estimate broadcast reach and frequency from tabulations and formulas.

Many researchers have made tabulations that show the reach achieved with different media schedules. These tabulations are put into formulas from which we can estimate the level of delivery (reach) for any given schedule.

Shown are the *reach curves* for typical schedules in two television segments: Nighttime and daytime. A reach curve is the technical term describing the graphic display of reach accumulation with increasing use of a medium.

If we schedule 200 GRPs in nighttime television, we would reach approximately 80 percent of women. Scheduled in daytime television, 200 GRPs would reach about 45 percent of women. Once reach is determined, we can obtain average frequency by dividing the GRPs by the reach:

$$\frac{200 \text{ GRPs}}{80 \text{ Reach}} = 2.5$$

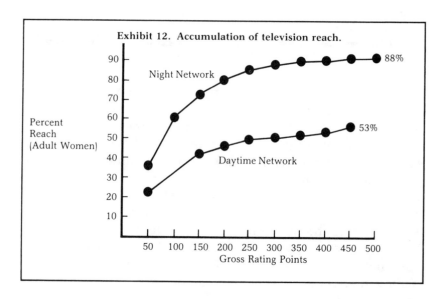

Exhibit 12. Accumulation of television reach.

The following tables demonstrate the reach and frequency estimates for varying levels of Gross Rating Points in television and radio. Bear in mind that reach/frequency are dependent to a large degree on scheduling patterns. In television, for example, concentration of commercials in a few programs will deliver more frequency and less reach. Conversely, a schedule encompassing a lengthy list of programs will tend to increase reach but deliver less frequency.

How to read: A schedule of 25 household GRPs per week (100 over four weeks) in daytime network TV will reach 43 percent of all households an average of 2.3 times each.

Table 12. Reach frequency at different GRP levels (TV).

Four-week Reach/Frequency

Audience Segment/ Weekly GRPs	Day Network	Prime Network	Late Night Network	Fringe Spot*
Households				
25	43/2.3	64/1.6	32/3.1	61/1.6
50	57/3.5	82/2.4	42/4.8	80/2.5
75	64/4.7	88/3.4	47/6.4	87/3.4
100	69/5.8	92/4.3	50/8.0	92/4.3
Women 18+				
25	41/2.4	60/1.7	28/3.6	57/1.8
50	54/3.7	76/2.6	34/5.9	75/2.7
75	61/4.9	83/3.6	38/7.9	84/3.6
100	65/6.2	88/4.5	40/10.0	88/4.5
Men 18+				
25	NT	59/1.7	25/4.0	56/1.8
50	NT	75/2.7	31/6.5	75/2.7
75	NT	82/3.7	34/8.8	82/3.7
100	NT	86/4.7	36/11.1	87/4.6

*Fringe spot is an equal mix of Early and Late Fringe.
NT-not tabulated.

It is important to note that the above table demonstrates the reach and frequency (R/F) for different *types* of GRPs: households, women aged 18 or older, men aged 18 or older. As discussed in the section on "Ratings," a rating can be calculated for homes or for people. A program with a 20 household rating will achieve a somewhat lower rating against total people, or men, or women, etc. Therefore, purchasing 100 household GRPs produces fewer people GRPs.

In radio, the same general dynamics hold true for reach, frequency and GRPs. The factors affecting reach and frequency in radio are: (1) the GRP level purchased; (2) the dispersion of announcements over different stations; and (3) the dispersion of announcements over different times of the day. The lower the number of weekly announcements per station, the greater the length of the station list purchased and therefore, with increased dispersion, the greater the reach.

How to read: If the media buyer purchased 25 "audience" GRPs per week and each station purchased aired nine announcements per week, the schedule would generate an R/F of 22/4.5 over a four-week period.

Table 13. Reach/frequency at different GRP levels (radio)			
	Four-week Reach/Frequency		
	Number of Announcements/Station/Week		
Weekly Audience GRPs	9	12	18
25	22/4.5	18/5.6	13/7.7
50	39/5.1	32/6.3	23/8.7
75	53/5.7	44/6.8	33/9.1
100	65/6.2	55/7.3	42/9.5

RATINGS FOR UNREPORTED AUDIENCE

The "audience" referred to in the above table can be any population segment for which data is available from syndicated sources. *Arbitron*, one such source, reports ratings for the following demographic segments:

Men, or women, or adults	18 and older
	18–34
	18–49
	25–49
	25–54
	35–64
Teens	12–17

Rating information can also be obtained for other population groups (for example, men 35–49), but there are two cautions involved. The first is that ratings, because they are a percent of a population base, cannot be added to or subtracted from each other. One cannot, for example, take a 10 rating for men 18–34 and subtract it from a 15 rating for men 18–49 to determine a rating for men 35–49. To make this calculation, one must deal with the absolute population and audience numbers, and perform the following arithmetic:

● Multiply the reported rating for each audience segment by the population base for that segment to find the absolute audience.

● Subtract the audience of the smaller segment from the larger to determine the audience for the demographic segment with no reported rating.

● Divide the audience obtained by the population base of that unreported segment to produce an average rating.

The steps are illustrated in Table 14.

Table 14. Calculating a rating for an unreported audience			
Audience Segment	Population Base	Reported Rating	Absolute Audience
18–49	1,000,000	15	150,000
18–34	400,000	10	40,000
35–49	600,000	—	110,000
	110,000 ÷ 600,000 = 18 rating		

The second caution involves the "stability" of the resulting rating and the basic data being used to calculate the new rating. As will be discussed later under the heading "Sampling Error," all rating information is based on the media consumption habits of a portion of the population and therefore can be affected by what happens in the *real* world.

REACH/FREQUENCY IN PRINT MEDIA

Because of the nature of the audience data collected by syndicated research companies, GRPs do not have to be used to estimate reach and frequency for print media.

Syndicated research companies, such as *Simmons* and *MRI*, collect readership information for a long list of publications. The data is also reported on the basis of *duplicated* readership—how many people read *both* Magazine A and Magazine B, *both* Magazine A and Magazine C, etc., as was demonstrated in Exhibit 7. These *duplication rates* are used in various mathematical formulas to determine the reach of combinations of magazines. The formulas are complex and usually require a computer program to accomplish the calculations. Most magazines have access to the computer programs, as do most advertising agencies, either through their own proprietary systems or through research service companies such as *Telmar* or *Interactive Market Systems*.

If duplication rates were reported for TV or radio programs, the same kind of formulas could be developed to calculate broadcast reach and frequency. The media planner would not have to rely on the generalities of GRPs and general audience accumulation data. However, because of the dynamic and ever-changing program environment in broadcast media, such duplication information would be relatively unreliable for predicting future media consumption patterns.

REACH/FREQUENCY IN OUT-OF-HOME MEDIA

With the exception of periodic national studies conducted by such companies as *Simmons Market Research Bureau* or the *Institute of Outdoor Advertising*, there is little specific data available to determine the reach and frequency of out-of-home media (such as outdoor or transit advertising).

A national study by *Simmons* revealed that in a thirty-day period a 100-GRP package in outdoor media reaches 87.2 percent of all adults in the average market, with a frequency of 24.9 times. Specifically, 100 GRPs in outdoor is the purchase of one or more poster panels, which will deliver in one day exposure opportunities equal to 100 percent of the population in the market.

HOW IMPRESSIONS ARE USED

Like Gross Rating Points, impressions also indicate *total* delivery without regard to duplication. Impressions are used to demonstrate delivery of alternative schedules.

Here, we have two plans at equal budgets. Both plans deliver 120 million *home* impressions. If we were interested only in homes, with both plans producing the same impressions, we would be hard pressed to select the better plan. If we were concerned with women, Plan I would be superior as it delivers more women impressions. If women 18–34 years old were of primary consideration, Plan II has the advantage.

Table 15. Comparison of alternative plans having equal expenditures.

| | Impressions (000) | |
	Plan I	Plan II
Total homes	120,000	120,000
Total women	90,000	85,000
18–34	30,000	40,000
35–49	30,000	30,000
50 & over	30,000	15,000

Another use for impression data is to compare the composition of a media plan's delivery to its objectives to determine if delivery is in the relative proportion desired.

As shown below, Plan I delivers impressions in a flat pattern—equal delivery to each age grouping. Plan II, with 47 percent of impressions accounted for by women 18–34, is biased to delivery to younger women and therefore more closely approximates the objectives of the media plan.

Table 16. Impression comparison of two plans.

| | Percent Total Impressions | | |
	Objective	Plan I	Plan II
Total women	100%	100%	100%
18–34	50	33	47
35–49	25	33	35
50 & over	25	33	17

A dilemma could arise if, when comparing alternative media plans, the planner finds that one plan delivers more impressions to the primary audience being sought, while the other media plan delivers fewer impressions to this group but a greater percentage of the *total* impressions. As Karl Malden might say in one of his American Express commercials: "What will you do?"

The answer is complicated, and at the same time easy. The reader should have a sense at this point in the book that many variables are involved in analyzing media forms and devising a media plan. No one variable (reach, frequency, impressions, etc.) should ever be the only criterion for decision making. Additionally, a number of methods exist for dealing with each of the variables in combination whereby a *valued* decision can be made. More about this later.

Frequency Distribution

Frequency distribution is the array of *reach* at each *frequency level.*

We have noted that during an advertising campaign people are reached with different *rates of exposure.* For example, when we spoke of magazine reach and frequency we saw that some people read only one magazine, some read two and some read three. This resulted in a frequency level of 1.0, 2.0 and 3.0, respectively. Further, the reach for each of these frequency levels was also shown—indicating that 24 percent of the people were exposed to the media *only* once, 11 percent *only* twice, and 4 percent *only* three times. That example illustrates the concept of frequency distribution.

In the advertising campaign illustrated below, 30 announce-

Table 17. Frequency distribution.

Schedule: Nighttime network TV—10 announcements
Daytime network TV—20 announcements

Frequency	Women Reach at Each Level
Only 1	23.7%
" 2	19.6
" 3	13.9
" 4	9.0
" 5	5.4
" 6	3.8
" 7	1.9
" 8	1.2
" 9	.7
10 or more	.8
Total reach	80.0%
Average frequency	2.8

ments were used in a combination of nighttime and daytime television. In total, 80 percent of women were reached with one or more exposures. The *average* woman reached was exposed to 2.3 commercials. The frequency distribution reveals that 23.7 percent of women were exposed to *only* one commercial, 19.6 percent to *only* two commercials, and so on.

Effective Reach

Effective reach is the number of individuals (or homes) reached by a media schedule *at a given level of frequency*. Effective reach is also commonly called *effective frequency*.

Although there is no definitive and universally accepted research which quantifies the value of each exposure level (i.e., how much greater is the advertising value of a consumer seeing four advertising messages versus two messages), judgment suggests that the values are different. Furthermore, because of the absolute costs of purchasing media, care should be taken not to spend more, or less, than is necessary to deliver advertising *effectively*.

Some research has been conducted about the relationship between frequency of exposure and advertising effectiveness. An Association of National Advertisers publication, *Effective Frequency: The Relationship Between Frequency and Advertising Effectiveness*, summarizes most of the industry research conducted in this area. The author, Michael J. Naples, draws twelve conclusions from his analysis of the research. The conclusions are listed below to reinforce the concept of effective reach (frequency):

1. One exposure of an advertisement to a target group consumer within a purchase cycle has little or no effect in all but a minority of circumstances.
2. Since one exposure is usually ineffective, the central goal of productive media planning should be to place emphasis on enhancing frequency rather than reach.
3. The weight of evidence suggests strongly that an exposure frequency of two within a purchase cycle is an effective level.

4. By and large, optimal exposure frequency appears to be at least three exposures within a purchase cycle.

5. Beyond three exposures within a brand purchase cycle, or over a period of four or even eight weeks . . . increasing frequency continues to build advertising effectiveness at a decreasing rate, but with no evidence of a decline.

6. The frequency-of-exposure data from this review strongly suggests that wearout is not a function of too much frequency per se.

7. . . . very large and well-known brands—and/ or those with dominant market shares in their categories and dominant shares of category advertising weight—appear to differ markedly in response to frequency of exposure from smaller or more average brands.

8. Perhaps as a result of the differing exposure environments of television dayparts, frequency of exposure . . . has a differential effect on advertising response by daypart.

9. . . . the amount of money a brand spends on advertising as a percent of total category advertising expenditures has a significant positive effect on brand users' purchase probabilities.

10. Nothing we have seen suggests that frequency response principles or generalizations vary by medium.

11. Although there are general principles with respect to frequency of exposure and its relationship to advertising effectiveness, differential effects by brand are equally important.

12. . . . the leverage of different equal-expenditure media plans in terms of frequency response can be substantial.

The reader may conclude that an analysis of media schedule alternatives based on *average* frequency can be misleading. Two different media plans might produce the same average frequency but perform completely differently in terms of delivering as many consumers as possible at a predetermined level of frequency. Therefore, whenever possible, media schedules should be analyzed according to frequency distribution, and values should be placed on varying exposure levels.

Once we determine the value of given exposure levels, plans can be evaluated based on *effective* reach. Two methods could be employed:

1. Determine the minimum level of acceptable (or effective) frequency. As shown in the frequency distribution example below, 25 percent of women will see *only* one message, 20 percent will see *only* two messages, etc. Cumulatively, 75 percent of women will see one or more messages, 50 percent will see two or more, etc. If the minimum acceptable level of frequency is judged to be two exposures, then alternative media plans should be evaluated on the basis of reaching women two or more times. Similarly, maximum levels of frequency can also be determined, and reach beyond that level eliminated from consideration or given a lesser importance.

Table 18. Method 1—frequency distribution.

Frequency	Women Reach	Frequency	Women Reach
1.0	25%	1 or more	75%
2.0	20	2 or more	50
3.0	10	3 or more	30
4.0	5	4 or more	20
5.0	5	5 or more	15
6.0	4	6 or more	10
7.0	2	7 or more	6
8.0	2	8 or more	4
9.0	1	9 or more	2
10.0	1	10 or more	1

2. Determine the value of each frequency level (or range of
   frequency). For example, it might be judged that women
   reached with 1.0–2.0 frequency have a value 25 percent
   below the average (an index of 75); women reached with
   3.0–7.0 have a value of 50 percent above average (an
   index of 150); and women reached with 8.0 or more frequency have a value 60 percent above average (an index
   of 160). By cross-multiplying the reach at each exposure
   level by the assigned value, and adding the products of
   each multiplication, we can establish the *valued* reach of
   a given media plan.

Table 19. Method II—valued reach.

Frequency Range	Women Reach (%)	Value Index	Valued Reach (%)
1.0–2.0	45	75	34
3.0–7.0	26	150	39
8.0–10.0	4	160	6
Total			79

Quintile Distribution

A quintile distribution is akin to a frequency distribution, but rather than displaying reach at each frequency level, it groups the audience reached into five equal parts and averages the frequency for each group.

Although quintiles will be discussed in this chapter, the same concept applies to any *equal divisions* of people or homes (e.g., tertile: one third; decile: one tenth).

All media forms attract people at different levels of exposure, ranging from those who are heavy consumers of the medium to those who are lightly exposed or not users of the medium at all. The same phenomenon usually occurs with product consumption—ranging from those consumers who buy and use significantly more of a product than the average person to those who do not use the product at all. It is not uncommon, for example, to see data which reports that 20 percent of the population account for 80 percent of a product's consumption.

Displayed is a quintile analysis for men television viewers. One-fifth of men (20 percent of the total population) view 44.7 hours per week, compared to the average weekly viewing for all men of 20.9 hours. For purposes of demonstration, let us assume that each one fifth of the population is one man. Therefore, if we add the viewing hours of each of these five men, we arrive at the equivalent of 104.1 hours. Dividing the 44.7 hours of the *heaviest viewing quintile* by the total of 104.1 hours, we determine that these heavy viewers account for 42 percent of all viewing.

Table 20. Television quintile analysis (total viewing—men).

Quintile	% U.S. Pop.	Average Hours of Weekly Viewing	% of Total Viewing
Heaviest	20	44.7	42
Next	20	26.4	26
Next	20	18.4	18
Next	20	11.3	11
Lightest	20	3.3	3
Total	100%	104.1	100%
Average	—	20.9	—

Source: W. R. Simmons

CALCULATING A QUINTILE DISTRIBUTION

To calculate a quintile distribution, we must first have a complete frequency distribution. Using this data, the total reach must be divided into five equal parts (in this example, one-fifth of the total 75 reach is 15 reach).

As reach accumulates to 15 as we progress through the frequency distribution, we can tabulate average frequency. As mentioned earlier, reach × frequency = GRPs. Therefore, to calculate the average frequency for each fifth of the audience reached, first determine the GRPs for each fifth of the audience; then divide the GRPs by the reach.

In the bar labeled "Heaviest" in Exhibit 13, the total GRPs were determined by multiplying reach × frequency for each frequency level: 5 × 6.0 plus 4 × 7.0 and so forth through 1 × 10.0. The total accumulated 110 GRPs, divided by the 15 reach, result in an average frequency of 7.3 for that quintile.

In this example, the most lightly exposed group has an average frequency of 1.0. The most heavily exposed group has an average of 7.3.

QUINTILE DISTRIBUTIONS OF A MEDIA MIX

Whenever a second medium is added to the first, the frequency distribution (and therefore the quintile distribution)

Exhibit 13. Television quintile analysis.

		Equal Fifths		Quintiles			
Frequency	Reach	Reach	Frequency	GRPs	Reach	Frequency	
1.0	20	15	1.0	15	15	1.0	Lightest
		5	1.0				
				25	15	1.7	Next
2.0	15	10	2.0				
		5	2.0				
				40	15	2.7	Next
3.0	10	10	3.0				
4.0	10	10	4.0				
				65	15	4.3	Next
5.0	5	5	5.0				
6.0	5	5	6.0				
7.0	4	4	7.0				
8.0	3	3	8.0	110	15	7.3	Heaviest
9.0	2	2	9.0				
10.0	1	1	10.0				
Total Average: 3.4	75	75		255	75	3.4	

flattens. Disproportionately more frequency is added to the more lightly exposed groups than to the most heavily exposed group.

There is a mistaken belief that heavy users of one medium are light users of another. This appears logical if one concludes that people, in general, spend about the same amount of time each day with their preferred media forms. Therefore, if people view television for most of that time, they will have less time to spend with other media. While logical, this is not a real-world phenomenon. The fact is that people spend varying amounts of time with media. Some are heavy consumers of media overall; some are light consumers. As a result of this pattern, consumers of one medium (e.g., magazine readers)

have an equal propensity to be heavy, moderate, or light consumers of another medium.

The logical and real-world assumptions are displayed in the
following two tables. Table 21 shows what might happen if
people, in general, spend about the same amount of time with
their preferred media forms. For example, most of the heavy
radio listeners would be light TV viewers. To read the chart: 20
percent of adults are considered *heavy* radio listeners. These
20 percent view television for varying amounts of time. Ten
percent of these 20 percent are *heavy* viewers, compared with
30 percent who are *light* TV viewers. At the other end of the
spectrum are light radio listeners. A large portion of these are
concentrated within the heaviest TV viewing quintile, i.e., they
tend to view TV more than they listen to radio.

Table 21. Hypothetical inter-media quintile distributions.

Radio Quintiles

% Adults	Heaviest 20%	Next 20%	Next 20%	Next 20%	Lightest 20%
Prime TV Quintiles					
Heaviest	10	15	20	25	30
Next	15	20	25	30	10
Next	20	25	30	10	15
Next	25	30	10	15	20
Lightest	30	10	15	20	25

Table 22 displays the real-world situation. It shows that
heavy radio listeners are almost equally distributed among
each of the TV quintiles. To read the chart: 20 percent of adults
are considered *heavy* radio listeners. Of this 20 percent, 19
percent are heavy viewers of primetime TV, and 23 percent
are light viewers. The same holds true for light radio listeners;
that is, 21 percent of all listeners are heavy TV viewers, and 20
percent are light TV viewers.

Table 22. Real-world inter-media quintile distributions.

	Radio Quintiles				
% Adults	Heaviest 20%	Next 20%	Next 20%	Next 20%	Lightest 20%
Prime TV Quintiles					
Heaviest	19	20	20	21	21
Next	19	21	20	20	19
Next	19	21	22	19	19
Next	19	20	21	20	20
Lightest	23	19	18	20	20

Source: Simmons, 1983

Because of what happens in the real world, the frequency distribution tends to flatten whenever a second medium is added to the first. Adding magazines to a base of television, for example, delivers equal frequency to each TV quintile but *disproportionately* more frequency to the lighter viewing quintiles than to the heavier viewing quintiles. As shown in Exhibit 14, the addition of magazines increases frequency among the lightest viewing fifth by 200 percent, compared with a 27 percent increase in frequency of the heaviest viewing fifth.

In this example, television provides a frequency of one to the lightest quintile, 1.7 to the next quintile, up to a 7.3 average frequency to the heaviest viewing quintile of reach. Magazines, with an average frequency of 2.0, deliver the same level of frequency to each of the TV viewing quintiles.

If additional television were scheduled in lieu of a second medium, the quintile distribution would have the same configuration as shown above for television alone. The absolute level of frequency would increase proportionately across each of the quintiles.

The same dynamics operate regardless of which two media forms are used. More of the same medium results in a quintile distribution that delivers significantly more frequency to the heavy consumers of that medium than to the lighter users. A

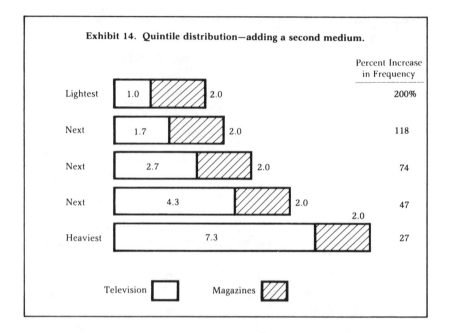

Exhibit 14. Quintile distribution—adding a second medium.

second medium always disproportionately increases the frequency among the lighter users of the first medium.

Quintile distributions are a better designator of frequency among different groups of people than average frequency but less discriminating than a complete frequency distribution. Nevertheless, quintile distributions are used periodically to assess the dynamics of a media schedule, to determine the impact of a second medium, or to decide when an additional commercial should be put into the pool of commercials being aired, etc. Judgment dictates how many exposures are sufficient, or too few, or too many.

Demography

Demography is the study of the characteristics of populations related to size, growth, density, distribution and vital statistics. Demographic analyses permeate marketing and media planning. Nearly all investigations of a brand's strengths and weaknesses, and a medium's strengths and weaknesses, involve a critical analysis of how *people* consume the product and "consume" media.

In order to make the right decisions in choosing specific media, the media planner must know who should be addressed in the media plan. The planner must also know to what extent different media deliver specific audiences—how many people of a particular population group view a television program, or read a magazine, or listen to a radio station, etc.

Demographic descriptions are available from many sources, not the least of which is the Bureau of the Census. The major syndicated media research companies (A. C. Nielsen, Arbitron, Simmons Market Research Bureau, Mediamark Research, Inc., etc.) all provide data on the basis of demographic "cells" (specified groupings of particular population groups, such as men 18–34, men in households with incomes of $20,000–$25,000, etc.).

Although demographic studies are important to the planning process, they are usually considered of secondary importance to studies that define product *users*, or users of products within a given category. An assessment of product users is a more effective method of analysis because media selection is predicated on the ability to reach very specific groups of people who are most apt to purchase a particular product or service.

A product user study can therefore give the planner a more precise definition of each medium's ability to reach these users. A demographic study, in this context, is an inference. To say that men 18–34 years old have an above-average propensity to buy tennis shoes does not mean all these men have the same propensity. The inference is, however, that if you advertise tennis shoes to this group of men you have an above average chance of reaching more of the men who actually do buy tennis shoes.

If user profiles are more useful than demographic profiles, the obvious question arises: Why aren't they used? There are four reasons:

- The first is tradition. Demographic profiles have been used for many years as the standard practice for defining media objectives and selecting media.
- Second, the various sources do not all define users, or do not define users in the same manner. If all media cannot be analyzed on the basis of their ability to reach users of a specific product, then the analysis by definition will be incomplete.
- Third, the reported information in the syndicated research sources is based on a sampling of the population. The number of people in the sample reporting usage of a particular product might be so few as to make the data reported unreliable.
- Fourth, not all products are reported by syndicated sources, nor all brands within a product category. New products, not on the market, of course, would not be reported until the products were purchased by consumers. This would make analysis impossible for those products not reported.

Index

An index is a percentage that relates numbers to a base. It is used to demonstrate quickly what is average, above average, or below average in terms of concentrations of people within predefined categories.

The category defined in this example is men who have played tennis in the past year. Hypothetically, we want to determine which of the age groups have the greatest concentrations of these men so we can properly select media to reach them. This procedure can be done in a number of ways, an *index* being one. The table below indicates there are 77.5 million men in the U.S., and 12.2 million (16 percent) who played tennis in the past year. Likewise, of the 15.0 million men in the U.S. aged 18–24, 5.4 million (36 percent) played tennis. We can readily see that there are *proportionately* more men aged 18–24 who played tennis than there are in the population at

Table 23. Calculating an index.

| Age | Total Men Population (Millions) | Men Who Played Tennis in the Past Year | | Index |
		(Millions)	% Total	
18–24	15.0	5.4	36	225
25–34	18.5	4.0	22	138
35–44	12.6	1.6	13	81
45–54	11.0	.8	7	44
55–64	10.2	.3	3	19
65 & older	10.3	.1	1	6
Total	77.5	12.2	16	100

large: 36 percent versus 16 percent. In going through long statistical tables, one could cite where there is a higher, average, or lower concentration by observation of each percentage.

The easier method is to calculate an index to determine the proportional relationships. By dividing the 36 percent by the 16 percent, we arrive at a quotient of 225 percent. The 225, without a percent sign, is the *index*. In this case it states there is a 125 percent greater concentration of men who played tennis in the 18–24 age group than is found in the general population. Note that the index includes the 100 percent representing the base:

Base (average)	100%
% increase	+ 125
Total (index)	225

An index of 100 indicates an average concentration (or average relationship). Indices over and under 100 indicate concentrations which are respectively higher or lower than average.

The index for men 35–44 years old is 81 (13 percent divided by 16 percent). The 81 indicates that this group is 19 percent below average:

Base (average)	100%
% decrease	− 19
Total (index)	81

To further demonstrate how an index works, we can take the problem one more step. If we assumed that 16 percent of *all* men, regardless of age, played tennis, we would have calculated that 2.4 million men aged 18–24 would be in this category:

Population (millions)	15.0
Percent who played	× 16%
Number who played (millions)	2.4

The actual data reveals that 5.4 million men 18–24 played tennis—3.0 million men more than assumed. If we divide the incremental 3.0 million men by the assumed 2.4 million men, we arrive at an increase of 125 percent. Adding back the base 100 percent, we come to an index of 225:

Actual Number Who Played (millions)	5.4
Assumed Number Who Played (millions)	− 2.4
Incremental (millions)	3.0

$$3.0 \div 2.4 = 125 + 100 = 225$$

or

$$5.4 \div 2.4 = \qquad 225$$

As shown in Table 23, it is perfectly valid to say that men 18–24 are the primary target because "they index at the highest level." Index alone, however, should not necessarily be the only factor in determining target groups. Consider, for example, that men 35–64 account for 2.7 million men tennis players, which is 22 percent of all men tennis players. By targeting solely to men 18–24, and assuming you are able to purchase media to reach only this age segment, you would be missing a substantial portion of all tennis players.

BRAND DEVELOPMENT INDEX

Indices are used to express any relationship of numbers within any category. Commonly, a Brand Development Index (BDI) is displayed by geographic area to show how each area is performing relative to the average U.S. performance. As shown in the following table, Markets A and D are above average, Market B on average, and Markets C and E below average.

The indices in Table 24 could be calculated in various ways and still yield the same conclusions. Method # 1 is to divide the percent of total sales accounted for in each market by the percentage of total population in that market:

Market A

$$\frac{\% \text{ Brand sales}}{\% \text{ Population}} = \frac{11}{10} = 110 \text{ BDI}$$

Table 24. Brand development index.

Market	% U.S. Population	% Brand Sales	BDI	Share of Market	BDI
A	10	11	110	22	110
B	15	15	100	20	100
C	20	18	90	18	90
D	25	30	120	24	120
E	30	26	87	17	87
Total	100	100	100	20	100

Method # 2 is to divide the "share of market" in each area by the average U.S. share of market. In the above example, this brand commands a 22 percent share of market in Market A—i.e., of all the product category sold in this market, this particular brand accounts for 22 percent of the total. The average market has a 20 percent share. Therefore, 22 share divided by 20 share equals a 110 index or a 110 BDI.

Cost-Per-Thousand (CPM)

CPM is an abbreviation of *cost-per-thousand* with the "thousand" from the Latin "*mille*." It is the cost-per-one-thousand individuals (or homes) delivered by a medium or media schedule.

CPM can be calculated for any medium, for any demographic group and for any total cost. It conveniently shows the *relative* cost of one medium to another, or one media schedule to another. It is not unlike the *cost-per-ounce* we now find in supermarket pricing.

We use CPM to evaluate alternative selections—yet another method in determining the best medium or media schedule. For example, we might be considering the purchase of either Program A or Program B, weighing the price to be paid in terms of the audience each is delivering. By dividing the cost of each program by the delivery of each program, we can determine the cost-per-unit of delivery:

$$11{,}500{,}000 \;\overline{)\;\$100{,}500.00\;} = \$.00874$$

If we multiply the cost-per-unit of delivery by 1,000, we arrive at a cost-per-thousand of $8.74: $.00874 × 1,000 = $8.74. On a calculator, the faster method is to eliminate three zeros from the delivery and perform the same division:

$$11{,}500 \;\overline{)\;\$100{,}500.00\;} = \$8.74$$

As shown, the cost for a 30-second commercial in Program A is $100,500. Program A delivers (is viewed by) 11,500,000 homes. The cost-per-thousand homes delivered is therefore $8.74. The CPM for men is $14.61 ($100,500 divided by 6,880,000 men).

A practical use of CPM is shown in the magazine comparisons in the table. We might be considering, for example, the purchase of either Magazine A or Magazine B. We find both costs and delivery for each magazine are different. By computing CPM for total women, we see both are equally efficient—both have the same CPM. However, if the media plan's objective is to emphasize delivery to women 18–49 years old, and we calculate CPM for this demographic, we find Magazine B is more efficient: Magazine B delivers women 18–49 at a lower cost-per-thousand readers.

Table 25. Calculating cost-per-thousand

		Viewers (000)		CPM	
	Cost/:30	Homes	Men	Homes	Men
Program A	$100,500	11,500	6,880	$8.74	$14.61
Program B	$ 96,500	16,700	9,660	$5.78	$ 9.99

		Readers (000)		CPM	
	Cost/Page 4-color	Women	Women 18–49	Women	Women 18–49
Magazine A	$64,600	17,460	11,900	$3.70	$5.43
Magazine B	$46,940	12,680	9,100	$3.70	$5.16

Cost-Per-Rating Point

The cost-per-rating point, or cost/GRP, is the cost of purchasing one rating point in broadcast media.

The primary function of a cost/GRP is to estimate the total cost of a planned TV or radio schedule within a market or nationally. For example, to determine how many GRPs are affordable within a given budget, divide the cost/GRP into the total budget. If your budget is $2,500 and you know that the cost/GRP for the type of schedule you wish to buy is $25, you are able to purchase 100 GRPs:

$$\frac{100}{\$25\ \overline{\smash{)}\ \$2,500}}\quad \text{GRPs}$$

The following table illustrates how cost/GRP and cost-per-thousand are related though quite different from each other. The table shows a TV household population in market X of 500,000. A 10 rated announcement will therefore deliver 50,000. The cost for this :30 announcement is $250, resulting in a cost/GRP of $25 and a CPM of $5. If you purchase 100 GRPs you deliver the equivalent of the TV household population in the market—500,000 homes. These 100 GRPs, at $25 cost/GRP,

Table 26. Interrelationship of cost/GRP & CPM.

	Market X		
	Homes	Cost	CPM
10 Rating	50,000	$ 250	$5.00
100 GRPs	500,000	$2,500	$5.00
Cost/GRP		$ 25	
TV Homes Base:	500,000		

will cost \$2,500. Dividing \$2,500 by the 500,000 impressions also results in a CPM of \$5.

Costs vary by market, by station within market, by the type of programming being purchased and by season. The media planner should therefore use the appropriate estimated cost/GRP when considering all these variations. The following table, for example, shows that the annual average cost/GRP in Market X is \$25. This varies through the year from a low of \$20 to a high of \$29 based on the demand and supply of TV advertising in each period. If the planner has a \$2,500 budget, on *average*, 100 GRPs can be purchased. This same budget spent in the July–September period will purchase 125 GRPs. Conversely, if the media plan calls for the purchase of 100 GRPs in this same period, the cost will be only \$2,000.

Table 27. Estimating affordable GRPs.

	Cost/GRP	Affordable GRPs for \$2,500	Cost for 100 GRPs
Annual average	\$25	100	\$2,500
Jan–Mar	\$24	104	\$2,400
Apr–Jun	\$27	93	\$2,700
Jul–Sep	\$20	125	\$2,000
Oct–Dec	\$29	86	\$2,900

Audience Composition

Audience composition is the percentage of individuals in each demographic cell.

Audience composition gives a clear indication of the concentration of audiences for each media vehicle. To this extent, it is not unlike the *reason* for calculating an index. The arithmetic, however, is different and much more straightforward. The inspection of audience composition data presupposes the question: "What amount of the total audience is my target audience?"

In Table 28 we see that two programs each deliver 50,000 viewers. Of the people who view Program A, 17,500 are men. These men represent 35 percent of all viewers (17.5 divided by 50.0). Women account for 40 percent of the audience, teens for 15 percent and children for 10 percent. Program B's audience composition is somewhat different, with proportionately more teens and children than men and women. It can be said that Program B *skews* (is biased) toward younger audiences.

Table 28. Audience composition.

	Program A		Program B	
	(000)	%	(000)	%
Men	17.5	35	15.0	30
Women	20.0	40	12.5	25
Teens	7.5	15	12.5	25
Children	5.0	10	10.0	20
Total	50.0	100%	50.0	100%

Audience composition varies dramatically by media category as well as among the specific media vehicles within a category. It is not surprising to find that movies, as a program type on television, have an audience composition similar to that of the population as a whole. Different movies, however, attract different audiences and the audience composition for a specific movie could be markedly different from that of movies in general. Similarly, *Sport* magazine and *Sports Illustrated*, both within the category of men's magazines, display different audience compositions.

One should not make generalizations about the *average* audience composition of any media grouping. Each media vehicle should be assessed independently of the others.

Geographic Areas

Most source material showing product sales or media delivery presents information on some territorial basis that allows the media planner to make evaluations based on geographical units rather than relying only on national data. This type of investigation leads to more precise media plans—plans that target not only demographic groups, but demographic groups within specific cities, states, etc. Here are the more common geographic units.

BROADCAST COVERAGE AREA

A broadcast coverage area is the geographic area within which a signal from an originating television station can be received.

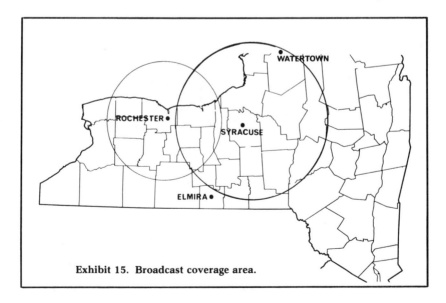

Exhibit 15. Broadcast coverage area.

A television signal is broadcast from a point of origin. As shown in Exhibit 15, TV stations originating in Syracuse can be viewed in an area extending from Watertown down to Elmira. People living in Yates County are within the broadcast coverage area of both Syracuse and Rochester stations.

TELEVISION MARKET

A television market is an *unduplicated* geographic area to which a county is assigned on the basis of the highest share of viewing of originating stations.

Both the A. C. Nielsen and Arbitron companies survey viewing habits in every county in the United States. This data reports how much the people in each county view each TV station. With this data, we are able to determine which stations are viewed most and then assign the county to one market or another.

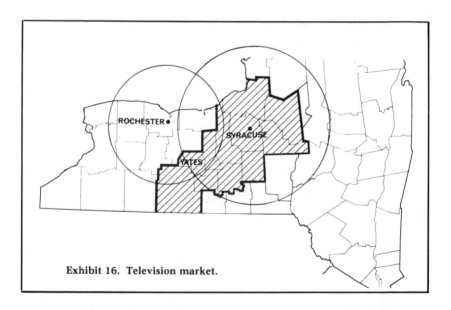

Exhibit 16. Television market.

The homes in Yates County view more hours of programs originating from Syracuse than they do programs coming from

Rochester stations. Yates County, therefore, is assigned to the Syracuse television market.

It is necessary to place a county in only one TV market to avoid an overlap of information. If a county were assigned to more than one television market, it would make geographic analyses of media delivery impossible. There are about 205 TV markets in the United States, which encompass over 3,000 counties. Arbitron's term for a TV market is Area of Dominant Influence (ADI); Nielsen's term is Designated Market Area (DMA). Although the terms differ, and to some extent so do the research techniques establishing viewing habits, ADI and DMA are quite similar, and both are synonymous with the term TV market.

Various data are often tabulated according to these designations, such as the demographic characteristics of the population (age, sex, income, etc.), purchasing patterns (food expenditures, gasoline consumption, etc.). Media consumption is also tabulated for the same geographic areas (television viewing, radio listening, magazine and newspaper circulation, etc.). Having all this data enables us to conveniently assess how to spend advertising budgets in each medium on a geographic basis.

RADIO MARKET

A radio market is generally referred to as either a Total Survey Area (TSA) or Metro Survey Area (MSA). Unlike TV markets, TSAs can overlap: a number of counties can receive originating radio stations from different cities. MSAs, however, do not overlap and are therefore used for buying purposes.

For a county to be part of the TSA, people living in the county must have established certain levels of listening to the radio station(s) broadcasting within their geographic area. These listening levels are tabulated from the survey diaries filled out by those in the survey sample. One listening level, for example, requires that a radio station be mentioned (listed) in at least ten diaries as being listened to for at least five minutes during any quarter hour within a survey week.

METROPOLITAN STATISTICAL AREA

Designated by the federal Office of Management and Budget, a Metropolitan Statistical Area (MSA) always includes a *city* (or cities) of specified population which constitutes the central city, and the *county* (or counties) in which it is located. An MSA also includes contiguous counties when the economic and social relationships between the central and contiguous counties meet specified criteria.

The basic criteria for an MSA are:

- It must include at least one city with 50,000 or more inhabitants, or an urbanized area of at least 50,000 inhabitants and a total metro area population of 100,000.
- It must have one or more central counties. These are the counties in which at least half the population lives in the Census Bureau urbanized area.

Counties which do not meet the above criteria could be included in an MSA if they satisfy other requirements. There must be significant levels of commuting from the outlying county to the central county (ies), and the county (ies) must display a specified degree of "metropolitan character" by meeting any one of the following conditions:

- Counties with a commuting rate of 50 percent or more must have a population density of at least 25 persons per square mile.
- Counties with a commuting rate from 40–50 percent must have a population density of at least 35 persons per square mile.
- Those with a commuting rate from 25–40 percent must have a population density of at least 50 persons per square mile, or at least 35 percent of their population classified as urban by the Bureau of the Census.
- Counties with a commuting rate from 15–25 percent must have a population density of at least 50 persons per square mile, and meet two of the following requirements:

    - Population density must be at least 60 persons per square mile.

- At least 35 percent of the population must be classified as urban.
- Population growth between 1970 and 1980 must be at least 20 percent.
- Either 10 percent or at least 5,000 persons must live within the urbanized area.

In addition to the designation of MSAs, the government has also defined two other geographic entities based on the 1980 Census:

> *Consolidated Metropolitan Statistical Area (CMSA).* This is the largest designation in terms of geographic area and market size. It is made up of component PMSAs that together total at least one million in population. These CMSAs, or *mega* areas, are usually of little use to marketers because of their prohibitive size. However, they exert some influence on bordering counties because of the proximity of potential buyers for area goods and services.

> *Primary Metropolitan Statistical Area (PMSA).* These are the component pieces that make up the CMSAs. They are directly associated with other PMSAs, but remain separate entities in terms of the socioeconomic data collected for them and presented in various research reports. To be classified as a PMSA, an area must be comprised of counties that conform to the following standards:

> - A total population of at least 100,000.
> - A population that is at least 60 percent urban.
> - Less than 50 percent of the resident workers commute to jobs outside the county.

Sales & Marketing Management magazine is a well-known primary source for collecting the government data and reporting meaningful marketing statistics for each of the metro areas shown above. On the basis of 1980 Census data, *S&MM* reports there are currently 315 metro areas in the U.S.

Many syndicated research sources delineate product category sales and media delivery by metro area, making geographic analysis convenient. We should keep in mind that a metro area is the hub of a television market, but does not encompass the entire population of the TV market. With 315 metro areas and 205 TV markets, the average metro area contains 1.5 TV markets.

NEWSPAPER AREAS

The Audit Bureau of Circulation (ABC) verifies member newspapers' total circulation statements and reports circulation on various geographic bases that aid the media planner in assessing precisely where the newspaper is distributed. Three geographic units are generally reported:

- **City Zone** is the area bounded by the corporate limits of the community in which a newspaper is published. Additional contiguous areas are included in the City Zone if these areas have the same characteristics as the community itself.
- **Retail Trading Zone** is the area beyond the City Zone whose residents regularly shop in the City Zone.
- **Primary Market Area** is defined by the newspaper publisher and is that area in which the publisher believes the newspaper has its greatest strength on the basis of readership, editorial coverage of the communities and advertising.

Based on ABC data, other research syndicators report circulation on a metro area and TV market basis.

NIELSEN COUNTY SIZE GROUPS

Nielsen County Size Groups are composed of counties assigned to one of four designations by A. C. Nielsen, based on population density and labor force concentration.

The specific definition of each county size group is as follows:

A   All counties belonging to the 25 largest MSAs.

B   All counties not included under "A" that either have
over 150,000 population or are in metropolitan areas of
over 150,000 population.

C   All counties not included under "A" or "B" that either
have over 40,000 population or are in metropolitan
areas of over 40,000 population.

D   All remaining counties.

County size is used to investigate urban/rural patterns of
sales and media delivery. Several syndicated sources show
sales as well as media delivery (such as magazine circulation)
on a county size basis. Quick assessments can be made about
the concentrations in the biggest cities ("A"), big cities ("B"),
smaller cities ("C") and rural areas ("D"). If sales for Product X
skew to "A" counties and Magazine Y has its highest penetration in "C" and "D" counties, then Magazine Y is probably not
a desirable medium.

County size investigations should be made as an adjunct to
television market analysis or in lieu of TV market data when
the latter is not available. For example, if we are estimating
potential sales for TV markets for which there is little or no
sales data available, we can assume that counties within the
TV market will perform by size as do the national sales by
county size.

Magazine Audiences

When we speak of magazine audiences, we generally mean *total* audience: The sum of all readers of a given issue regardless of how they received the magazine, where it was read, or to what extent it was read. There are different types of readers who are generally grouped as follows:

Primary Readers—Those readers in the household in which the magazine was *purchased.*

Passalong Readers—Those readers not in the primary household.

In-Home Readers—Primary or passalong readers who read the magazine in their own home.

Out-of-Home Readers—Primary or passalong readers who

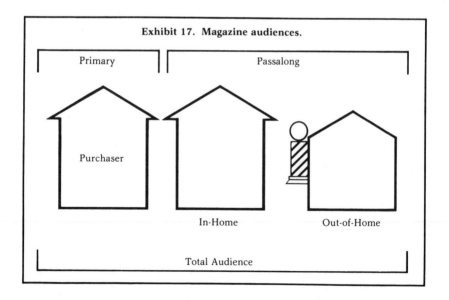

Exhibit 17. Magazine audiences.

read the magazines outside of their home: At work, on airplanes, in doctors' offices, etc.

There are studies (Alfred Politz, Elmo Roper) that indicate a greater value for the in-home versus the out-of-home reader. The in-home reader spends more time with the magazine, picks it up more often and receives more satisfaction from it than the out-of-home reader. This, combined with some basic logic, reveals that the out-of-home reader, for most magazines, should be devalued. Many advertising agencies currently put the value of the out-of-home reader at 50 percent that of the in-home reader.

Not all magazines' out-of-home audiences should be devalued. For example, *Industry Week* magazine is specifically edited for business executives who generally read the publication at their workplace. Also, in-flight publications reach a captive reader who probably spends as much time reading the average page as does the in-home reader of a mass monthly publication. *People* magazine commissioned a media research study to demonstrate that their out-of-home audience spends as much time reading their publication as do their in-home readers because of the nature and layout of their magazine.

Table 29. Readership by place of reading.

		Percent of Adults Reading		
	Total	In Own Home	Out of Own Home	At Work
Better Homes & Gardens	100	64	36	8
Fortune	100	41	59	31
TV Guide	100	87	13	2

Source: MRI, Spring, 1984

Patterns for in-home and out-of-home readers vary by magazine depending on the type of magazine and the reading convenience. A high percentage of *Better Homes & Gardens* readers read in their own homes—a convenient place to think of home furnishings and gardening editorial. *Fortune* readers are concentrated more out-of-home, mostly at work, which is a more convenient place to react to business information. *TV Guide*, used primarily as a television program listing, is obviously read mostly at home.

Readers-Per-Copy

Readers-per-copy is the total number of primary and pass-along readers of a given issue of a publication. By multiplying readers-per-copy by the circulation of an average issue, we can arrive at *total audience*.

Several factors affect the number of readers-per-copy a magazine will garner:

- **Distribution Patterns.** Circulation in areas with high potential audience, such as airplanes, doctors' offices, etc., allows more people to be exposed to a specific copy of the magazine.
- **Amount of Editorial.** Physically, the more words contained in a magazine, the longer it takes to read. The primary reader will therefore hold the copy longer with fewer pass-along readers having the opportunity to see that issue (e.g., *Reader's Digest*).
- **Type of Editorial.** Some publications have a tendency to be retained by the primary reader because of the reference material in the magazine (e.g., *Nation's Business*), the reproduction quality (e.g., *National Geographic*), for visual display in their library (e.g., *Architectural Digest*), or any number of other reasons.

It takes time for a magazine to accumulate its total audience. A magazine usually is not passed along until the first reader has read it. Additionally, some readers do not begin reading a magazine until well after they buy it or receive it.

As can be seen in table 30, weekly magazines, such as *People* and *Time*, accumulate their total audience within five weeks of their issuance, while monthlies, such as *McCall's* and *Reader's Digest*, do not accumulate their total audience until ten weeks after they are issued.

Table 30. Percent total women readers accumulated.

Week	People	Time	McCall's	Reader's Digest
1	56	64	41	45
2	81	87	65	65
3	92	95	76	80
4	98	98	84	90
5	100	100	89	95
6			93	97
7			96	98
8			98	99
9			99	99
10			100	100

Source: IMS

These are some of the basic assumptions that researchers make when they assess magazine audience accumulation:

- The shorter the publication interval, the faster the accumulation.
- The higher the readers-per-copy, the slower the accumulation.
- Timely or news-oriented publications are consumed faster and therefore accumulate faster.
- The higher the percentage of newsstand circulation, the more rapidly the primary audience is accumulated.
- The larger the percentage of in-home audience a publication has, the faster its audience accumulation.

Audience accumulation varies by type of reader. The primary reader has the first opportunity to read a given issue of a magazine and primary audiences are, therefore, accumulated faster. An independent research firm (SORTEM) conducted studies among primary and passalong readers which showed, for example, that among the four women's service magazines studied, 43 percent of the magazine's primary audience read the issues within the first week compared to only 15 percent of the magazines' passalong audience. Similarly, in-home audiences (which tend to have heavy concentrations of primary readers) are accumulated faster than out-of-home audiences.

Table 31. Variations in audience accumulations.
(Percent audience accumulated)

	Time Magazine		
Week	Total Audience	In-Home Audience	Out-of-Home Audience
1	64	76	40
2	87	95	70
3	95	100	85
4	98		95
5	100		100

Source: SMRB 1978/79; IMS

If immediacy of delivery is an important consideration in the media plan, or the timing of the advertising campaign is critical, the planner should bear in mind the differing audience accumulation patterns that exist for different publications.

Broadcast Dayparts

Broadcast dayparts are the time periods in a 24-hour day during which television and radio programs are broadcast.

In television, there are *basically* seven dayparts. The exact times vary by time zone and sometimes from market to market.

Table 32. Television dayparts.

General Time Period
(EST)

Daytime	10:00 a.m.–4:30 p.m.	Monday–Friday
Early evening	4:30 p.m.–7:30 p.m.	Monday–Friday
(or early fringe)	5:00 p.m.–7:30 p.m.	Saturday & Sunday
Prime access	7:30 p.m.–8:00 p.m.	Monday–Sunday
Primetime	8:00 p.m.–11:00 p.m.	Monday–Saturday
(or nighttime)	7:00 p.m.–11:00 p.m.	Sunday
Late night	11:00 p.m.–1:00 a.m.	Sunday–Saturday
(or late fringe)		
Weekend children's	8:00 a.m.–2:00 p.m.	Saturday & Sunday
Weekend afternoon	2:00 p.m.–5:00 p.m.	Saturday & Sunday
(incl. sports)		

As shown in Exhibit 18, each daypart attracts different audiences because of the programs being telecast as well as the availability of viewers. Men are less available during the daytime TV hours, therefore women account for the lion's share of viewers. This fact remains true despite the increase of working women who are less available to view daytime TV. Late evening TV programming attracts adult viewers, the majority of them young adults. Saturday morning programs are viewed primarily by children, whereas programs telecast during weekend afternoons attract proportionately high levels of men viewers.

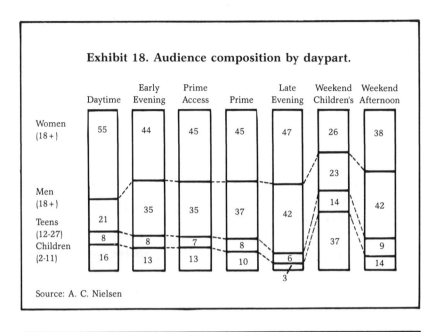

Exhibit 18. Audience composition by daypart.

	Daytime	Early Evening	Prime Access	Prime	Late Evening	Weekend Children's	Weekend Afternoon
Women (18+)	55	44	45	45	47	26	38
						23	
Men (18+)		35	35	37	42	14	42
Teens (12-27)	21						
Children (2-11)	8	8	7	8		37	9
	16	13	13	10	6		14
					3		

Source: A. C. Nielsen

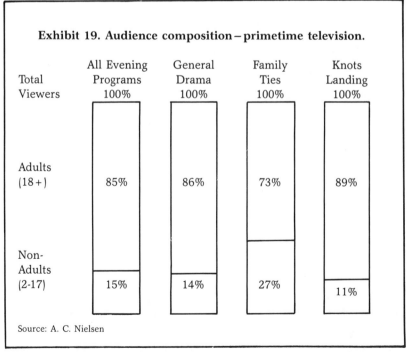

Exhibit 19. Audience composition – primetime television.

Total Viewers	All Evening Programs 100%	General Drama 100%	Family Ties 100%	Knots Landing 100%
Adults (18+)	85%	86%	73%	89%
Non-Adults (2-17)	15%	14%	27%	11%

Source: A. C. Nielsen

As stated earlier (see Audience Composition), generalities can be misleading. There are wide variations in the demographic composition of the viewers by program within dayparts.

Exhibit 19 displays audience composition for primetime TV comparing the average of all programs to general drama programs, and to two specific general drama shows. As a category, general drama has about the same composition as the average of all evening programs. "Family Ties," however, has a proportionately younger audience, while "Knots Landing" has a proportionately older audience.

Radio has essentially four dayparts.

Table 33. Radio dayparts.

	General Time Period (EST) Sunday–Saturday
AM drive (or primetime)	6:00 a.m.–10:00 a.m.
Daytime	10:00 a.m.–3:00 p.m.
PM drive (or primetime)	3:00 p.m.–7:00 p.m.
Nighttime	7:00 p.m.–Midnight

As with television, audience composition varies by daypart (Table 34), and by programming type within dayparts (Table 35).

Table 34. Radio listenership.

(Percent of total listeners by daypart)

	Monday–Friday			
	Men (18+)	Women (18+)	Teens (12–17)	Total (12+)
AM drive	42	51	7	100
Daytime	43	52	5	100
PM drive	42	47	11	100
Nighttime	40	44	16	100

Source: Radar

Table 35. Audience composition of radio by programming format.

Percent of Total Listeners by Age

	12–17	18–24	25–34	35–54	55+	Total	Median Age
Contemporary, Top 40, Disco	33	25	23	16	3	100	22
Rock	27	44	22	5	2	100	23
Classical Music	2	9	18	34	37	100	45
Country Music	4	7	18	34	37	100	47
Middle-of-the-Road	4	5	13	37	41	100	49
Good Music	2	5	13	38	42	100	50
News	3	7	12	34	44	100	51
Talk	1	5	8	33	53	100	56

Source: *The Media Book*

Broadcast and Cable Media

NETWORK TV

A network is any group of stations joined to broadcast the same programs—usually simultaneously.

There are three television broadcast networks: ABC, CBS and NBC. The stations affiliated with these networks contract to air a certain amount of network programming each week—usually about 55–60 hours. In return, they are paid a compensation, or fee.

The number of stations that any one entity can own (corporation, partnership, individual, etc.) is limited by the Federal Communications Commission. No more than 12 AM radio stations, 12 FM radio stations and 12 TV stations can be owned by one entity. Additionally, the combined coverage of the stations cannot exceed 25 percent of the U.S. TV homes. UHF TV stations count only as half of a market's TV homes for purposes of this calculation. A group can own up to 14 of each kind of broadcast station, with a maximum U.S. TV homes coverage of 30 percent, but only if two of each kind of station are controlled by minorities.

Each of the three TV networks *own and operate* (O&O) five TV stations, as shown in Table 36. The five stations combined currently account for about 20 percent U.S. TV household coverage for each of the three networks.

ABC, CBS and NBC are called "line networks" because they have the capacity of transmitting programming from New York or Hollywood via telephone lines for simultaneous exposure across the U.S. They may also send videotapes of programs to stations for airing at different times in different markets. When a network program in a local market airs at a different time or on a different day from the original telecast, it

Table 36. O & O stations.

	ABC	CBS	NBC
New York	WABC	WCBS	WNBC
Chicago	WLS	WBBM	WMAQ
Los Angeles	KABC	KCBS	KNBC
Philadelphia	—	WCAU	—
St. Louis	—	KMOX	—
Cleveland	—	—	WKYC
Washington	—	—	WRC
Detroit	WXYZ	—	—
San Francisco	KGO	—	—

is termed a "delayed broadcast" or "DB." These three networks also have the capacity to transmit programming via satellite.

Network television can be purchased in a number of dayparts any day or night. The programming varies from one daypart to the next, from season to season, and, often in primetime, from week to week.

Exhibit 20. Network television dayparts.

Time	Monday-Friday	Saturday	Sunday
6 A.M. 7 8	Early Morning Network		
9 10 11 12 Noon 1 P.M. 2	Daytime Network	Children	Information
3 4 5		Sports	Sports / Public Affairs
6 7	Network News	News	News
8 9 10 11	Primetime	Prime	Prime
12 Midnight 1 A.M.	Late Night	Late Night	
2 3 4 5 6	News		

CABLE TV

A number of *cable networks* also transmit programming and commercials to local markets by satellite. The local cable operator receives the signal via a disc antenna ("earth station") and retransmits it to subscribers in the local community. Some of the networks which accept advertising are:

> ESPN (Entertainment & Sports Programming
>   Network)
> CNN (Cable News Network)
> SIN (Spanish International Network)
> USA Network
> CBN (Christian Broadcasting)
> MTV (Music Television)
> Nickelodeon
> Lifetime
> FNN (Financial News Network)
> The National Network
> CNN Headline News
> Arts & Entertainment

SUPERSTATIONS

Lastly, four TV stations commonly referred to as "Superstations," operate in the U.S. They are independent stations whose signal is transmitted locally via normal broadcast and nationally via satellite:

> WTBS (Atlanta)   WGN (Chicago)
> WOR (New York)   WPIX (New York)

NETWORK RADIO

In radio, there are 14 line networks:

> ABC Contemporary   CBS Radio Radio
> ABC Direction   Mutual
> ABC Entertainment   NBC
> ABC FM   NBC Source
> ABC Information   NBC Talk Talk
> ABC Rock   RKO I
> CBS   RKO II

A station affiliated with, or owned by, ABC that has a contemporary music format is part of the Contemporary network, while a station with a news/talk format belongs to the Information network.

Table 37. Network radio O & Os.			
	CBS	ABC	NBC
New York	WCBS (am)	WABC (am)	WNBC (am)
	WCBS-FM	WPLJ (fm)	WYNY (fm)
Los Angeles	KNX (am)	KABC (am)	—
	KKHR-FM	KLOS (fm)	—
Chicago	WBBM (am)	WLS (fm)	WMAQ (am)
	WBBM-FM	WDAI (fm)	WKQX (fm)
St. Louis	KMOX (am)	—	—
	KHTR-FM	—	—
Philadelphia	WCAU (am)	—	—
	WCAU-FM	—	—
San Francisco	KCBS (am)	KGO (am & fm)	KNBR (am)
	KRQR-FM	—	—
Detroit	—	WXYZ (am)	—
	—	WRIF (fm)	—
Boston	WHTT-FM	—	—
	WEEI-FM	—	—
Washington	—	WMAL (am)	—
	—	WRQX (fm)	WKYS (fm)
Houston	—	KSRR (am)	—

RADIO STATION GROUPS

In addition to radio line networks, there are several Radio Station Groups. These stations do not air programming or commercials over the telephone lines. They are "unconnected" stations that offer a group discount on the advertising rate which would normally be paid if the stations were purchased separately. Although these group networks have the potential of covering the entire U.S., they can be purchased market-to-market to tailor a media buy geographically. The groups are:

McGavren Internet   Blair Radio Network
Torbett Supernet   Keystone Network
Katz Radio Group

When you buy TV or network radio, you buy a fixed line-up of stations that will cover a specified percentage of the U.S. The delivery (ratings) in each market, however, varies according to:

- The difference in viewers'/listeners' tastes;
- The local (non-network) programming scheduled opposite the network program;
- Delayed broadcasts;
- Non-clearance—the program is not carried in that market.

SPOT TV

Spot buying refers to the purchase of commercial time on a market-by-market, non-network basis on either network affiliated stations or independent stations (not affiliated with a line network).

As opposed to network buys, spot purchases can be made on any station in any market. The number of markets purchased may range from one to all in the U.S. and the number of announcements can vary from one market to the next.

Announcements can be purchased in locally originated programs, between network programs (called "break positions" or "adjacencies") and, in some instances, within a network program. Network program positions are limited to specific nonsponsored hour shows and some movies. There are also a few occasions when a network has unsold time which is turned back to its affiliated stations for local sale. These units are called co-op minutes or thirties.

PARTICIPATION/SPONSORSHIP

A participation has two definitions depending on the medium purchased:

- The purchase of an individual announcement in network television, usually as part of a package of "scatter" announcements purchased without commitment to full or partial sponsorship agreements.
- In spot buying, an announcement appearing within a program as opposed to the break.

Sponsorship of a program usually requires a majority purchase of the announcements available within a program or a program segment. Sponsoring advertisers are generally given one or more "billboards" at the beginning and/or end of the program. Billboards announce program sponsorship to the audience and afford the advertiser free, albeit brief, advertising.

SYNDICATION

Syndication is a method of placing a program on a market-by-market basis as opposed to the line interconnected or satellite connected systems of program transmittions. Placement may be made by independent producers, by advertisers, by advertising agencies or syndication companies. A syndicated program may be of any type, any duration, and may be telecast at any time of day or evening.

Syndicated programs usually air in the early fringe or prime access time periods (non-network time periods) when they air on network affiliated stations. When airing on independent stations they may appear anytime within the broadcast day depending on the discretion of the local station. Syndicated sports programs, for example, generally air on weekends while off-network properties such as "Lassie" are placed weekdays in early evening. The syndicator and the local station negotiate for a fixed time period.

Commercials can be placed in a syndicated program, depending on availability, in one of two ways:

- As a normal spot purchase, market by market.
- In the full line-up—a commercial in every market carrying the program.

Some syndicated properties are purchased by advertisers under terms in which the advertiser retains ownership for a number of commercial units (e.g., 2 minutes), gives the program to local stations gratis, and allows the local station to sell the remaining commercial units (e.g., 4 minutes) usually to non-competing advertisers.

NAB Code

The National Association of Broadcasters established *The Television Code* and *The Radio Code*. The purpose of the codes was to maintain a level of programming that gave full consideration to the educational, informational, cultural, economic, moral and entertainment needs of the American people. Although the federal government eliminated the NAB Code in 1982 on the basis of antitrust considerations, many broadcasters continue to observe the code's guidelines—either specifically or within the spirit of the code.

The code specified guidelines for airing non-program material in terms of content, number of interruptions within programs and the number of commercials that could be aired within each interruption. Non-program material includes billboards, commercials and promotional announcements. Table 38 indicates the acceptable limits that were established for the amount of non-program material aired on radio and TV.

Table 38. NAB Code (amount of non-program material).

	Amount	Program Length (Minutes)
Television		
Network affiliated stations		
Primetime	9 mins., 30 secs.	60
Other dayparts	16 mins.	60
Children's Sat./Sun.	9 mins., 30 secs.	60
Children's Mon./Fri.	12 mins.	60
Independent stations		
Primetime	7 mins.	30
Other dayparts	8 mins.	30
Radio		
All times	18 mins.	60

In addition to the amount of non-program material, the code also suggested the number of interruptions permitted within programs. These guidelines are shown in Table 39.

Table 39. NAB Code (number of television program interruptions).

Network Affiliated Stations	Number of Interruptions	Program Length (Minutes)
Primetime	2	30
	4	60
	2/half hour	longer than 60
	5	60 variety show
Children's	2	30
	4	60
Any time	1	5
	2	10 or 15

No more than 4 non-program material announcements shall be scheduled consecutively within programs and no more than 3 non-program announcements during station breaks.

Independent Stations

Stations not carrying a commercial in a station break:

Any time	4	30
	7	60
	10	90
	13	120

Stations carrying a commercial in a station break:

Any time	3	30
	6	60
	9	90
	12	120

Many believe that increased advertising clutter reduces the impact and memorability of advertising commercials. This phenomenon is exacerbated with the increased use of shorter length commercials, such as the :10 I.D. Advertisers who share this belief seem to have preferred stations which were code subscribers and favored them in media selection.

National/Local Print Media

Magazines can be purchased nationally, regionally or locally.

The larger national magazines often offer opportunities for purchasing less than national circulation in predetermined geographic areas (for example, the Northeast, or the state of Florida, or the Chicago metropolitan area). Additionally, many magazines circulate only in defined areas, such as *Sunset* magazine on the West Coast, or innumerable local magazines designated only for specific cities.

Some national magazines also offer demographic editions for purchase. An advertiser could buy space that runs only in copies directed to particular audiences (e.g., doctors only, businessmen only).

Newspaper supplements are also available for national or local purchase. For the most part, these supplements are distributed in the Sunday editions of local newspapers. There are two nationally syndicated supplements, *Family Weekly* and *Parade*, both of which produce one editorial package each Sunday, distributed by local newspapers throughout the U.S. The masthead of each newspaper is imprinted on the supplement.

Newspapers are primarily local in distribution, though there are national availabilities, such as *The Christian Science Monitor, The Wall Street Journal* and *USA Today*.

Besides the commonly known daily newspaper, with editions in the morning, evening or throughout the day, weekly newspapers are also available. Weekly newspapers tend to be smaller circulation periodicals distributed in smaller towns, or the suburbs of larger cities. The editorial and news emphasis in weekly newspapers is primarily local. Although this description applies generally to most suburban newspapers, many are increasing substantially in circulation and editorial coverage and some are beginning to have daily circulation.

Outdoor

Outdoor media can be purchased almost everywhere in the continental U.S. in any configuration of national or local placement. Indeed, outdoor is the most local of all general media forms inasmuch as one advertising unit can be purchased in one specific geographic area.

There are a vast number of out-of-home media availabilities ranging dramatically in size and location. Only the more popular varieties of media vehicles will be discussed here.

Poster panel—This is an outdoor advertising structure on which a preprinted advertisement is displayed.

The most widely used posters are the standard poster panels designated as "bleed," "30-sheet" or "24-sheet." The sheets refer to the number of pieces of paper originally needed to cover the panel area. At one time, posters were printed in 24 pieces, but with today's larger presses, the 24-sheet poster is usually printed in 10 to 18 pieces.

A bleed poster is designed to utilize the entire posting surface. An acceptable size is 10′5″ by 22′8″, whereas a 30-sheet poster generally has a copy area approximately 9′7″ high by 21′7″ long.

The junior panel poster (sometimes referred to as a "6-sheet" or "8-sheet") is approximately one-fourth the size of the standard poster panel and mechanically is a direct adaptation of a 30-sheet poster. The "3-sheet" poster, however, is a vertical display, usually 82″ high by 40″ wide.

Showings—Posters are generally sold in combination in order to achieve a predetermined level of exposure within a market. These levels are expressed as "showings" of different sizes, such as #100 showing, #50 showing, etc. Showings are synonymous with Gross Rating Points generated within one day. Therefore, a purchase of a #100 showing should achieve a daily circulation (i.e., potential exposure) equivalent to the population of the market in which the posters are purchased. Showings are generally purchased on a monthly basis.

Painted bulletins—These are outdoor advertising structures on which advertising is directly painted.

Paints are generally larger than posters, averaging a copy area of 14' by 48'. There are two varieties of painted bulletins:

- **Permanent,** on which advertising remains fixed at one location for the duration of the purchase contract.
- **Rotary,** in which the display face is physically moved to a new location within the market at stated intervals—usually every 30, 60 or 90 days.

Permanent paints are sold by the individual unit on a one-year basis. Most paints are usually given priority placement in a market and therefore generate higher levels of traffic (auto as well as pedestrian) as well as having greater visual impact than posters. This, combined with the fact that paints are more costly to produce, results in paints costing significantly more to purchase than posters.

Rotary painted bulletins can be purchased individually or in packages where all locations are changed periodically with no location being used more than once. The type of purchase depends on the availability in a market and/or the advertiser's requirement.

Transit

Transit advertising is available in selected cities on buses, taxi cabs, trains and in carrier terminals (train stations, airline terminals, etc.)

The more commonly used units are:

- Car cards on the interior of buses or trains, usually measuring 11" by 28" up to 11" by 56".
- Busoramas, which are back-lighted displays appearing on the rooftops of buses.
- Clock spectaculars, the elements of which are a large clock and an accompanying back-lighted display, generally found in carrier terminals.
- Front end displays, placed on the fronts of buses measuring approximately 21" by 44".
- King-size posters displayed on the sides of buses, filling an area about 2' by 12'.
- One-sheets, found on train station platforms and measuring about 46" by 30".
- Two-sheets, same as one sheets but twice as large.
- Rear-end displays, placed on the back of buses and usually measuring 21" by 72".
- Taxi cab displays, which vary in size and type by market.

Most transit advertising is sold by showing size: A number of posters displayed on different vehicles or station platforms throughout a given transit system. Inside transit advertising, such as car cards, is bought on the basis of full, half and quarter showings. A full showing places a display in every vehicle of a fleet; a half showing in half the vehicles; and a quarter showing in every fourth vehicle. Outside transit displays are purchased on the same basis as poster panels, i.e., #100, #50, etc.

OTHER OUT-OF-HOME MEDIA

This is a catch-all category for displays that are not considered posters, painted bulletins or transit advertising.

There are sandwich boards, shopping cart displays, shopping mall displays, airplane tows, sky-writing, and on and on and on.

Among the relatively new media forms are video advertising, silent radio and screenvision. Video advertising, located primarily in shopping malls, consists of proprietary programming transmitted via satellite to television monitor displays. Silent radio consists of digital L.E.D. "broadcasts" of news, sports and weather which are transmitted via a radio signal to the physical units located mostly in retail establishments (eg. restaurants). A tradition in Europe for many years, screenvision has been recently imported to the U.S. The medium enables advertisers to reach a younger audience with long commercial commercial messages (up to three minutes) on movie theatre screens.

Sampling Error

All media research is based on a sampling of the total population, a representative group whose media and product consumption patterns supposedly replicate those of the whole population, or those of a specified portion of the total population. Inherent in using a sample rather than the entire population is "sampling error"—the possible deviation of the reported finding from what might be the actual finding had the entire population been studied.

Making media decisions based on small differences among alternatives is therefore a shaky process. The planner must keep sampling error in mind whenever numerical comparisons among alternative media solutions are made because, in the real world, the exact opposite of what the research says *could* be true.

A.C. Nielsen's Network Television Service reports ratings for all nationally televised programs based on a sample of approximately 1,680 homes. The TV sets in these homes have Audimeters attached to them which electronically record when the sets are turned on and to which program. On an average day, about 1,450 homes record usable data. These sample homes represent the viewing patters of 85 million TV homes in the U.S.

For a typical weekly program, Table 40 shows the range in ratings that could be expected at each rating level. For example, if Nielsen reports a program received a 20 household rating, the standard sampling error is plus or minus 2.2 rating. This program's actual rating could therefore range from a low of 17.8 to a high of 22.2—an 11 percent variation (relative error) from the reported rating.

A program with a 15 household rating could, in the real world, have been viewed by 16.8 percent of the population, and

Table 40. Sampling error.

Household Rating	Error +/−(*)	Rating Range	Relative Error
5	1.2	3.8 – 6.2	24%
10	1.6	8.4 – 11.6	16
15	1.8	13.2 – 16.8	12
20	2.2	17.8 – 22.2	11
30	2.4	27.6 – 32.4	8
40	2.6	37.4 – 42.6	7

*At 95% confidence level.

a program with a 20 rating by 17.8 percent of the population, making these two programs only one percent apart in actual audience.

A sampling error exists in every research report that relies on a sampling of the population rather than on the entire population to gather its facts. By understanding this limitation, the planner or buyer can use research more as a *guideline* for decision making than as the final word.

The following table demonstrates the possible decisions which might be made to purchase either radio station A or B.

Table 41. Application of sampling error in purchase decisions.

	Station A	Station B
Average Quarter-Hour Rating	3.8	1.1
Men listeners (000)	57.0	16.5
Cost/Announcement	$114	$35
CPM	$ 2.00	$ 2.12
Sampling Error ±	.7	.4
Possible Rating		
Low	3.1	.7
High	4.5	1.5
Possible Men Listeners (000)		
Low	46.5	10.5
High	67.5	22.5
Possible CPM		
Low audience	$ 2.45	$ 3.33
High audience	$ 1.69	$ 1.56

On the surface, Station A appears to be superior with a lower CPM ($2.00 versus $2.12 to deliver men listeners with one announcement). However, when the sampling error is considered, we see that Station A could, in the real world, have only 46,500 men listeners while Station B could have as many as 22,500 men listeners. If we recalculate CPM based on these audiences, we find that Station B *could have* a lower CPM than Station A ($1.56 versus $2.45).

PART II
HOW TO CONSTRUCT A MEDIA PLAN

Overview

As a science, media planning requires the establishment of a hypothesis and a test of the variables that can prove or dismiss the hypothesis. The media plan, however, often does not evolve past the point of a theory. It can seldom be proven that a given plan is necessarily the *best* plan.

Much of media planning is judgment—informed judgment based on knowledge of the mechanics of each medium and some empirical evidence of how consumers react to media—but, nevertheless, judgment. Many of the decisions made on how to spend millions of advertising dollars are predicated more on convictions than provable facts. Many critical questions remain unanswered. Experience and good marketing/advertising judgment fill in the gaps.

We do not know, for example, how often a consumer must see an advertising message for Product X before the consumer buys Product X. And yet, the rate of exposure to advertising is one of the most important factors in devising a media plan. Exposure rate, or *frequency*, determines to a great extent which specific media are best, and how much money is necessary to do an effective job.

Despite a lack of crucial data, media decisions must be and are made. To guide the media planner in making correct decisions (more appropriately, practical and logical decisions which are agreed to by the advertiser), a structure is sought. We call this structure a media plan.

BASIC COMPONENTS OF A MEDIA PLAN

Planning involves essentially three basic activities. First, *defining the marketing problem*. Do we know where our business is coming from and where the potential for increased business lies? Do we know the markets of greatest importance and greatest opportunity? Do we know who buys and who is most likely to buy? Do we need to stimulate trial or defend a franchise? Do we need to reach everybody or only a selective group of consumers? How often is the product used? How much product loyalty exists?

The second basic activity is *translating marketing requirements into actionable media objectives.* If the marketing objective is to stimulate trial among all potential consumers, then reaching many people is more important than reaching fewer people more frequently. If the product is purchased often, then reaching people more frequently might be a more appropriate tactic.

The third basic activity is *defining a media solution* by formulating media strategies. If reaching people is a primary objective, one should select affordable vehicles that will generate more reach than other media forms. If a specific demographic group is to be reached, media selection should be based on reaching that group effectively and efficiently.

Some might argue with the definitions of objectives and strategies and prefer to call strategies "tactics," etc. But these are arguments based on semantics. The intent of formulating objectives and strategies is to have a course of action with disciplined thinking, and if this is accomplished, any phraseology can be used.

Media Objectives

The objectives of any media plan define *media goals*. The goals must be positive, action-oriented statements representing an extension of the marketing objectives and, therefore, also be marketing-goal oriented.

The objectives cannot be innocuous. They must position the media plan relative to the market and the marketing plan. An objective that states:

> Introduce Product X in order to achieve high levels of awareness.

does not provide direction. It says: Advertise. A more realistic and actionable objective guides the planner in assessing alternatives, such as:

> Reach at least 80 percent of the potential market within the first month of advertising, ensuring that the average consumer will be exposed to a minimum of four advertising messages.

Or

> Direct advertising to current and potential purchasers of Product Y by weighting current purchaser characteristics 60 percent and potential purchaser characteristics 40 percent.

INFORMATION REQUIRED

A. Marketing Objectives

Because a media plan is an integral part of the marketing plan, the media objectives must reflect the marketing objectives. For example, we must ask if the product needs high levels of advertising that command the consumers' attention (as with new products) or sustained advertising (as with established brands). Should advertising be scheduled in markets where the brand has its highest or lowest share? Are consumer promotions to be supported with advertising? Should media efforts be targeted to brand users, or non-users?

B. Marketing Research

Marketing research can help define the market and the consumer. There are a number of research resources available, such as Nielsen, Simmons and MRI, to help with this investigation.

C. Creative Strategy

Creative strategy must be considered. If color is mandatory, the media planner would be hard pressed to rationalize the use of radio. The need for long copy versus short copy, or the knowledge that one advertisement will be created versus a pool of commercials, all have a bearing on media selection.

D. Promotion Strategy

The planner must be aware of the promotion strategy and, where appropriate, coordinate media activity with promotional programs. If consumer coupons are to be used, the planner must know timing and distribution requirements. How many coupons? How often? What kind of redemption is planned? What areas of the country? What target group of consumers?

E. Sales Data

Sales data are often a must. No brand has a flat sales picture in all of the U.S. There are always areas of high and low development—areas where certain local factors or competitive forces play on the vitality of a brand. Sales data will also reveal seasonal sales patterns that may be important in scheduling advertising. The planner must also look at sales trends geographically. Seldom do the sales of a product increase or decrease in every market in the same way. Aberrations can usually be found and therefore acted on.

F. Competitive Activity

Competitive activity must be fully understood. The planner must analyze competitive efforts and ascertain: Which media are being used? How often? In which areas of the U.S.? To what levels? Investigating competitive media investment could reveal opportunities for dominating media not used by competition, or suggest increased spending in media used extensively by competition.

BASIC QUESTIONS

The best approach to formulating media objectives is to answer basic questions that encompass the general areas of audience, geography, scheduling requirements, copy needs, reach and frequency and testing.

1. Audience

Whom does the brand want to reach?
What is the relative importance of each group?

A thorough objective recognizes the importance, or lack of importance, of each demographic cell. The planner should analyze audiences on the basis of age, sex, income, education, race, employment status, family size, marital status, possessions, life style characteristics and any other traits for which data are availale. One must take care to ensure the creative strategy addresses the same people as defined in the media objectives.

There are usually one or two key demographic groups for most products or services, for example, women 18–34 years old. Too often, however, a planner analyzes this group alone, completely disregarding all other groups. By limiting analysis in this manner, he or she makes the conscious decision that groups not analyzed have zero value, and that media reaching these nondefined groups are providing unwanted delivery. It

behooves the media planner to analyze all demographic characteristics, including race, to set values for each group and
thereby determine a target audience that encompasses *all*
people.

Most market research generally reports on the value of each
cell within a demographic category, such as women aged
18–34 within the category of age. But very little research is
available to help in the decision of assigning values to each
category, such as the value of age compared to that of income
levels. If we do not place values on each category, then we have
made the decision that each category is of equal importance.
Logic dictates this is usually not the case.

An action-oriented objective providing clear direction to the
planner might read:

Direct media to demographic groups in accordance with current consumption patterns:

	Percent of Total Consumption
Women 18–34	30%
Women 35–49	20
Women 50+	10
Men 18–34	20
Men 35–49	15
Men 50+	5
Total	100%

As stated earlier, demographic studies are important to the
planning process, but are usually considered of secondary
value to studies that define product *users*. Whenever user data
is available to select media, it should be used.

2. Geography

Where should the brand concentrate its advertising efforts?
Are there markets which have minimal sales
and how should one value these markets?

Are brand sales changing disproportionately in any markets?

Is national advertising mandatory?

The planner should establish geographic targets for the smallest possible universe. In order of desirability, targets should be based on:

- Neighborhood
- County
- Market (metropolitan area, TV market, etc.)
- Sales area
- State
- Region
- County size

The planner should recognize the sales or sales potential in each geographic area as well as any other ingredient deemed important, such as income, housing, mobility, etc. Often, we can use related data as a predictor of product sales: Automobile mileage can be used to predict tire sales; temperature can be used to forecast sales of hot weather soft drinks.

It would be beneficial to establish a target for each geographic denominator and then allocate media delivery to each in accordance with these targets. Quite often it is necessary to do extensive sales analyses to establish targets by market.

Once all pertinent information is amassed, we need to decide which of two philosophies will be used to allocate advertising. There are two basic philosophies:

- **Advertise where the business is.** This is basically a defensive posture. It protects the existing franchise and simultaneously seeks to develop more business on the assumption that increases in brand sales can be achieved most efficiently where the brand is currently strong. It is easier to build on an existing base where product distribution has been established and where there is apparent consumer awareness and acceptance of your product. Current non-users in these areas have a greater propensity to become users than non-users in areas where your product sales are low.

- **Advertise where the business is not.** This philosophy is offensive. It is based on the belief that changing consumer demands, as well as changes in product formulation for your brand or the competitive brands, result in brand-switching. Advertising in these areas would therefore announce your presence and keep your brand on consumers' minds should they decide to switch brands. To implement this philosophy successfully, you must first ensure other marketing factors: You must have the right product for the consumers, competitive pricing, widespread distribution, sufficient inventory position to restock for repurchase after initial trial, and good display. Advertising alone will not produce sales, nor remedy marketing deficiencies.

One can use either philosophy, or some combination of both, depending on the marketing strategy. In any case, the objective at this stage of the analysis is to assign a "target percentage" to each market in the U.S. The target represents the *share* that market should receive of the total advertising effort. The target percentage for all markets combined must equal 100 percent.

3. Scheduling

> To what degree should the brand recognize seasonal sales patterns?
> Are there any discernible patterns?
> How important is the introductory versus the sustaining period?
> Should competitive advertising efforts be countered?

The planner must formulate precise direction for each of these areas. Whenever possible, you should use the most specific calendar units (days, weeks, months). The extent of any effort must be quantified in order to show emphasis clearly. For example, clear direction is shown in the following kinds of objectives:

> Spend advertising dollars in accordance with the percentage of sales each month.

Allocate no more than 60 percent of advertising expenditures during the introductory 13-week period.

Increase advertising activity by 50 percent during each of the three planned promotion periods. Precede the promotion by one week and run concurrently during the remaining four weeks of the promotion.

Concentrate all advertising from Wednesday to Saturday in order to reach potential Product X buyers immediately prior to the highest usage day, Sunday.

4. Copy

What are the basic requirements for color, audio, visual?
How does the complexity of the message affect copy length?
What is the brand's creative experience?

Copy is obviously of extreme importance to any viable advertising effort. Regardless of the impact of the media plan, if it does not properly reflect the copy strategy, the entire campaign suffers. The media planner should not, however, be the mistress of the copywriter. It is important for both to work together to create the best copy in the best medium, and this should happen in the early stages of planning. The copywriter should be made aware of the media ramifications of certain decisions as should the media planner have a complete understanding of the copy needs.

5. Coupons

Will the media plan require a consumer promotion in the form of a media distributed coupon?
How many coupons will be distributed?
How much reach will be required?

A number of advertising plans contain a promotional effort that can be either trade- or consumer-oriented. Trade promotions could take many forms, such as in-store displays, cost allowances (discounts) for purchasing certain quantities of product or purchasing at certain times of the year, sales contests, etc. These kinds of trade promotions do not generally require a consumer media effort.

A promotion directed to the consumer does require media support. Although the label of this effort is promotion, as opposed to advertising, the two must work in concert. If the marketing objective requires distribution of a cents-off coupon in order to counter competitive efforts or promote consumer trial, then this must be translated into an actionable media objective so the media planner can schedule appropriate media to deliver these coupons into the consumers' hands.

6. Reach and Frequency

> What reach level is needed?
> How much frequency is required?
> Should reach/frequency levels vary by market?
> Should reach/frequency levels vary by time of
> the year?

The number of people you need to reach with advertising, and how often you need to reach them has the most demonstrable effect on a media plan. If it is possible to have a precise objective that clearly establishes how many people need to be reached and how often, this will significantly influence your choices of which media forms to consider, how much of each medium can be used, the number of weeks that advertising is affordable, or the budget that is necessary to achieve this objective.

Unfortunately, this objective is sometimes written after a plan is constructed and the delivery of that plan is determined. While this guarantees the objective will be achieved and will thereby make the media planner a genius at the task, it is a pointless exercise. If a predetermined level of advertising intensity is desirable or needed based on past performance, competitive pressure or judgment, then the planner should state that level in the objectives—*prior* to devising the actual media plan.

7. Testing

Should a media or copy test be conducted?
What information can be garnered with a test?

Testing should always be considered in every media plan. There are too many unanswered questions to avoid testing. When one considers that an average media or copy test represents a negligible part of most large advertising budgets, the obvious conclusion is that testing should be continuous. Regardless of the media plan recommended, there is always room to conduct a test. For example:

- An unused medium—magazines if you are using TV, or radio if you are using magazines.
- Media mix—magazines and TV versus either alone, or radio plus newspapers.
- Copy length—ten-second commercials if the plan calls for :30s, or half pages instead of full pages.
- Scheduling—flighting advertising with hiatus periods as opposed to continuous advertising, or concentrating in one television daypart rather than dispersing announcements through two or more dayparts.

Representative areas of the U.S. should be carved out in which to conduct testing. The areas should not only be a microcosm of total U.S. demography, but should also be representative of average product consumption, as well as having appropriate media availability in which to conduct the test.

Finally, you should give the test a fair chance to work. There is no magic timetable for a test after which period you can draw valid conclusions. But it is fair to assume that a media or copy test conducted in the marketplace will take weeks, or months, or perhaps a year before its thrust is felt at the consumer level.

In some cases, not all objectives can be realistically met. For example, there may be an objective to reach at least 80 percent of a target group, and a second objective which requires advertising continuously throughout the sales season. Media availability and cost could prohibit the planner from accomplishing both of these objectives. It is therefore wise to give priorities to the objectives in order to have a clear direction in the decision-making process. If reach is given a greater priority than continuity of advertising, then the planner, when faced with the above situation, can elect to provide the needed levels of reach for as long a period as is affordable without necessarily advertising throughout the sales season.

SUMMARY

Media objectives define the media goals and should be action-oriented.

The best way to define objectives is to answer questions that have a bearing on media selection and usage.

Objectives should be established *before* the media plan is written . . . even if the plan recommended does not meet every objective precisely.

Testing on a continuous basis can lead to answering critical questions pertinent to the brand.

Media Strategies

Media strategies are the solutions to the media objectives. Strategy statements reflect specifically the course of action to be taken with media:

- Which media will be used
- How often each will be used
- How much of each medium will be used
- During which periods of the year

Devising media strategy requires that the planner have an in-depth knowledge of media characteristics—how they work, how they are consumed, how they can be used to generate a desired effect. The planner must also have an understanding of the media marketplace—what the availability and cost structure of each medium is at a given point in time. If the planner decides primetime network television should be scheduled for April to achieve a particular objective, he or she must know if the television networks have unsold inventory for this month and, if so, what the cost of these commercial units might be.

A number of media alternatives are available to achieve media objectives. The planner's job is to find the best medium, or combination of media, that will produce the best overall effect relative to the needs of the advertised brand. This requires extensive analysis.

The following are examples of how the planner might approach media analysis in order to accomplish several specific objectives. In all cases, the examples are illustrative of a particular situation and should not be construed as the only way to approach media analysis. Additionally, all examples restrict consideration to one or two audience segments and a few media alternatives. Actual analysis of media alternatives would require far more extensive tabulating than presented in these examples.

1. Target Audience Objective

Let us assume we have established an objective to recognize the relative importance of men and women in the purchase decision of Product X:

> Select media on the basis of a 40%/60% weight-
> ing for men and women respectively.

For illustration ease, let us also assume that the creative units available for this advertising effort are :30 television commercials, :60 radio commercials and full-page four-color magazine advertisements.

The first step in investigating which media might best suit the objective is to analyze the audience composition of the various media in order to establish a general idea of how each medium distributes its audience. The following exhibit shows, for example, that the average primetime network adult audience is composed of 43 percent men and 57 percent women.

Table 42. Audience composition.

	Men	Women	Total Adults
Television			
Primetime	43%	57%	100%
Daytime	21	79	100%
Radio	47	53	100
Magazines			
General	42	58	100
Women's	14	86	100
Men's	78	22	100

This overview would indicate that the exclusive use of daytime television would probably not achieve the objective because only a small portion of its adult audience is composed of men. Likewise, the exclusive use of men's magazines would be deficient in delivering women.

As stated in Part I, we should analyze audience composition for the specific media vehicles within broad categories. Audience composition varies widely among vehicles within a general category. The analysis, therefore, should include television program types, radio program types and specific magazines so the planner can seek out opportunities that might be masked by generalities.

The second step is to analyze the various media on the basis of actual delivery and cost efficiency. The higher the affordable level of delivery, the lower the cost-per-thousand. Higher absolute delivery will also result in increased reach and/or frequency.

The following table shows the gross impressions for each media form for men, women and total adults.

Table 43. Gross impressions affordable with a $1 million budget.

	Millions of People		
	Men	Women	Total
Network TV			
Primetime	79.9	106.3	186.2
Daytime	79.9	292.3	372.2
Network Radio	319.4	354.4	673.7
Magazines			
General	199.2	269.8	469.0
Women's	49.5	315.9	365.4
Men's	188.5	52.0	240.5

In order to accomplish the objective, however, the audience delivery must be weighted as stated: 40% men/60% women. By multiplying the men impressions of each medium by 40 percent and the women impressions by 60 percent, and then adding the products, "weighted" impressions can be established. Inasmuch as the impressions are devalued for each audience segment, the weighted impressions are not "real" numbers, but merely an indication of the *relative* delivery of each medium.

Having established weighted impression delivery, the cost-

Table 44. Weighted delivery 40% men/60% women.		
	Impressions (Millions of People)	CPM
Network TV		
Primetime	95.7	$10.44
Daytime	207.3	4.82
Network Radio	340.3	2.94
Magazines		
General	241.6	4.14
Women's	209.3	4.78
Men's	106.6	9.38

per-thousand can be calculated for each media form. (See Table 44.)

Based on cost-per-thousand, the media planner would assign priorities to the media shown in this example as follows:

1. Radio
2. General magazines
3. Women's magazines
4. Daytime TV
5. Men's magazines
6. Primetime TV

Not all media have the same "communication value." Television, for example, is an instrusive medium—commercials are broadcast into a person's home without invitation. Some argue that this intrusive quality is advantageous because the consumer does not have to seek out the advertising. Others might argue that magazines offer advertisers the opportunity for full copy exposition in high fidelity color which the reader can refer to again and again.

Whether based on research data or judgment which considers the copy execution or competitive position of the brand, it behooves the planner to assign a weight to each medium that represents the medium's relative ability to communicate the message effectively. If medium X is considered to be only half as effective as medium Y, then medium X should be given a weight of 50, and medium Y a weight of 100.

The following table further weights the impressions shown in this exercise, using *hypothetical* values for each media form. For example, 207.3 million impressions for daytime network TV times a value of 75 percent equals *valued* impressions of 155.5 million.

Table 45. Valued impressions				
	Gross Impressions			
	Value ×	Weighted =	Valued	CPM
Network TV				
Primetime	100	95.7	95.7	$10.44
Daytime	75	207.3	155.5	6.43
Network Radio	50	304.3	170.2	5.88
Magazines				
General	75	241.6	181.2	5.52
Women's	75	209.3	157.0	6.37
Men's	75	106.6	80.0	12.50

At this point, the planner has evaluated all media on the basis of their ability to deliver a weighted target audience of 40% men/60% women, and has further weighted each medium on the basis of communication values. Based on a cost-per-thousand ranking (with the lowest CPM being the first choice), the planner would have assigned the following priorities to each media form:

	Unweighted	*Weighted*	*Valued*
Network TV			
Primetime	6	6	5
Daytime	3	4	4
Network Radio	1	1	2
Magazines			
General	2	2	1
Women's	4	3	3
Men's	5	5	6

If cost-per-thousand were the sole criterion in selecting media, the first dollar spent should be allocated to general magazines. General magazines should be used to the level deemed appropriate before network radio is added to the media schedule.

Cost-per-thousand alone, however, should never be the sole criterion in selecting media. Before being able to make an intelligent media choice, one must consider many other factors, such as reach, frequency of exposure, reach accumulation over time, competitive efforts, promotional needs, etc. No media plan should have but one objective which requires only the achievement of delivering gross impressions at the lowest cost-per-thousand.

Nevertheless the above is useful as one ingredient in an analysis of media alternatives. When additional analyses are made which address the other objectives of the media plan, the planner can then evaluate the various media options in terms of achieving all objectives combined with the best alternative.

2. Geographic Objective

Another objective in a media plan might be to allocate advertising dollars to each market in the U.S. in proportion to sales.

There are usually pronounced differences in a brand's sales, competitive pressures, distribution penetration and a host of other marketing variables market to market. It's beneficial to use these pieces of data to allocate advertising to *each* market relative to local market phenomena.

The planner must first make a complete geographic business analysis which includes all pertinent marketing information. At minimum, this analysis should include product sales, but it usually includes other factors affecting sales and sales potential.

The assumption at this point is that the general media forms being used in the plan have already been selected: Television, magazines, newspapers, radio, outdoor, etc. The decision to be made is how much *national* media (e.g., network TV) and how much *local* (e.g., spot TV) should be used. The objective is to fit the delivery of the media to the local market targets.

The easiest way to match advertising delivery to pre-established goals in each market is to use only local media forms: Spot TV, spot radio, newspapers, outdoor, etc. The use of national media (e.g., network TV) would result in a mismatch in a number of markets. National media deliver their messages at different levels throughout the U.S. and almost never in proportion to the targets established for your brand.

As shown in the following exhibit, ten primetime TV announcements will deliver 94 men GRPs in the *average* market. GRP delivery will vary from market to market because of differences in viewing patterns—in this example, delivery ranges from a high of 107 GRPs to a low of 66 GRPs.

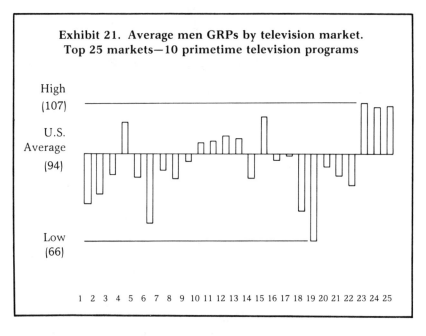

Exhibit 21. Average men GRPs by television market.
Top 25 markets—10 primetime television programs

High (107)

U.S. Average (94)

Low (66)

1 2 3 4 5 6 7 8 9 10 11 12 13 14 15 16 17 18 19 20 21 22 23 24 25

Looking at national magazine circulation, we again see wide variations from one geographic area to another. As shown in the following table, for example, *Reader's Digest* delivers 14.9 percent of its circulation in the Mid-Atlantic territory, compared to a population count of 17.6 percent. If you wished to deliver circulation in direct proportion to population, *Reader's Digest* (as well as other magazines) would not achieve your goal. Some areas would receive proportionately more circulation than you wished while others would receive less.

Table 46. Magazine circulation by geographic area.

Percent U.S. Circulation

Nielsen Territory	% U.S. Pop.	Reader's Digest	Time	Playboy
New England	5.7	5.6	8.7	5.7
Mid-Atlantic	17.6	14.9	20.3	15.1
E. No. Central	18.8	19.7	18.5	18.4
W. No. Central	7.9	9.7	7.4	8.6
So. Atlantic	15.8	14.7	13.7	14.5
E. So. Central	6.1	5.3	3.0	4.0
W. So. Central	9.7	9.4	6.3	9.2
Mountain	4.5	5.8	5.2	6.3
Pacific	13.9	14.9	16.9	18.2
Total U.S.	100.0	100.0	100.0	100.0

National media can be used, however, without overdelivering any market if the extent of their use is limited. The trick is to combine the proper levels of both national and local media so as to obtain optimum results in both local markets and for the U.S. as a whole.

Either of two methods can be used to allocate national and local media to local markets:

- **Dollar Allocation.** This method apportions the total *dollar* spending of all media combined to each market relative to the target percentage. If Chicago is targeted to receive 6 percent of the total U.S. investment, then 6 percent of your total media budget should be spent in Chicago.

- **Impression allocation.** This method allocates the total *impression delivery* of all media combined to each market, again relative to the target percentage. If Chicago is targeted at 6 percent, it should receive 6 percent of the media plan's total impression delivery.

The methods are based on two distinct strategies and produce significantly different results.

- **The dollar allocation system:**
    —matches sales dollars with advertising dollars.
    —equalizes return on investment in each market.

—limits spending in inefficient markets, thus producing more impression delivery overall.

—presupposes that *dollars* should be controlled without specific regard to the levels of advertising delivery in each market.

• **The impression allocation system:**

—produces an unequalized dollar investment in each market.

—does not relate advertising dollars to sales dollars.

—produces fewer impressions overall.

—produces impressions (or GRPs) in each market in proportion to the market's target.

—presupposes that consumers react to advertising delivery not dollars per se.

When purchasing national media, we assume that the investment in each market is in direct proportion to the delivery in that market: All markets therefore have the same cost-per-thousand. A package of 10 primetime network TV announcements costs approximately $1,000,000 and will deliver 94 men GRPs on a national basis, equal to 79,860,000 men impressions. The men cost-per-thousand of this package is $12.50. We have already established that GRP delivery varies from market to market. Therefore, to establish the number of impressions in each market, we need to multiply the local market GRP delivery by the TV base in that market. By then multiplying the local market impressions by the *national* CPM, we establish the prorated cost for a national plan in each market. In the following table we see that New York, with 6,177,000 men impressions, accounts for $77,300 of the $1,000,000 plan.

The same dynamics apply to the allocation of network radio dollars to each local market: Apportion total U.S. expenditures proportionately to each local market on the basis of local market impression delivery. In print media, the average national cost-per-thousand is applied to each market based on local circulation.

Once local market spending is established for national media forms, various combinations of national and local media can be analyzed to determine the optimum combina-

Table 47. Allocating network TV spending to local markets.

	Men Impressions (000)	CPM	Total Cost
New York	6,177	$12.50	$77,300
Los Angeles	4,300	12.50	53,800
Chicago	2,857	12.50	35,800
Philadelphia	2,857	12.50	29,300
San Francisco	1,925	12.50	24,100
Remaining Markets	62,265	12.50	779,700
Total U.S.	79,860	$12.50	$1,000,000

tion: That combination which will meet local market *targets* and deliver meaningful levels of advertising in each medium being used.

The following table shows two different media plans: Plan I is composed of only network TV; Plan II is a combination of network and spot TV. Both have the same $350,000 budget to be spent in three markets combined. The strategy in the media plan dictates that advertising expenditures should be in direct

Table 48. Dollar allocation.

Plan I—only network TV

	% U.S. Sales	Impressions (000)	CPM	Expenditures	% Total
A	50	28,000	$5.00	$140,000	40
B	30	28,000	5.00	140,000	40
C	20	14,000	5.00	70,000	20
Total	100	70,000	$5.00	$350,000	100

Plan II—network TV & spot TV

	% U.S. Sales	Target Budget	Network	Spot	Total	% Total
A	50	$175,000	$ 70,000	$105,000	$175,000	50
B	30	105,000	70,000	35,000	105,000	30
C	20	70,000	35,000	35,000	70,000	20
Total	100	$350,000	$175,000	$175,000	$350,000	100

proportion to sales in each market. Market A, therefore, should receive 50 percent of all dollars since it accounts for 50 percent of sales. Using the dollar allocation system, we determine that Plan I spends 40 percent of the total budget in Market A—underdelivering the 50 percent goal. Market B is overspent. Plan II, however, limits the spending in network TV to allocate the remaining funds to spot TV in the proportions needed to produce the proper overall spending pattern. As shown, Plan II expenditures by market are in direct proportion to sales.

There are obviously situations where underspending in a local market would be tolerated: In those instances where certain markets, regardless of their sales potential, are excluded from advertising consideration for any number of reasons or where the level of national advertising to be purchased is below minimum acceptable criteria. Overspending in a local market can also be tolerated under certain situations (e.g., when prior commitments to national media force the investment).

The procedures used for an impression allocation are similar to those of the dollar allocation. The planner calculates impressions for the total of all media being used and apportions them to each market based on local viewing/reading habits. The national delivery is subtracted from the target delivery to yield the number of impressions one needs to purchase via local media in order to meet the target. Local media impressions delivery is priced to determine affordability within the total media budget. Nearly always, the total target impression delivery costs more than the budget allows. You therefore need to make a prorated adjustment in each market to bring the total advertising plan within budget.

3. Scheduling Objective

Every media plan should have a scheduling objective to guide the planner in allocating media across the year. *When* advertising is delivered is often a critical issue. Advertising for suntan lotion should obviously be concentrated in those months when people need suntan lotion. Advertising for a product consumed to varying degrees throughout the year, however, presents a less obvious scheduling requirement. As stated earlier, you must make a complete investigation of the brand's needs vis-a-vis its competitive position and historical sales trend. These marketing considerations can be translated into actionable media objectives that will address, in broad strokes, the general requirement for the timing of advertising across the year.

Beyond the general timing consideration, the media planner should also consider the strategy of *flighting* versus *continuous* advertising. Some definitions:

> **Flighting** refers to periodic waves of advertising interspersed with periods of total inactivity.
> **Continuous** advertising is a schedule with little or no variations in pressure.
> **Pulsing** is a combination of the above two concepts: A continuous base of support augmented by intermittent bursts of heavy pressure.

Exhibit 22 demonstrates the three techniques by showing the number of weekly GRPs that can be scheduled using each pattern. All three techniques encompass a total of 1,200 GRPs over a 12-week period.

Audience accumulation of flighted and continuous schedules at equal rating levels is identical over the *long run*. All three schedules will accumulate the same number of Gross Rating Points (assuming equal costs during the entire advertising campaign period); all three schedules will reach the same number of people with equivalent frequency; all three schedules will distribute impressions among the different audience segments in about the same manner.

Audience accumulation of flighted and continuous schedules, however, will vary considerably over the *short run*. As shown in this frequency distribution (based on the flighted and continuous schedules shown in the exhibit 22), the flighted schedule produces slightly higher total reach (1 + frequency) over a four-week period than the continuous schedule, but substantially more reach at the higher frequency levels. If the media planner establishes an "effective reach" level of at least

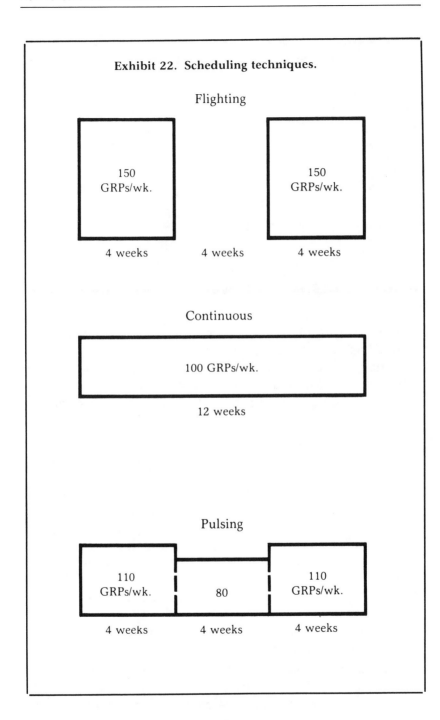

Exhibit 22. Scheduling techniques.

Flighting

150
GRPs/wk.

150
GRPs/wk.

4 weeks   4 weeks   4 weeks

Continuous

100 GRPs/wk.

12 weeks

Pulsing

110
GRPs/wk.

80

110
GRPs/wk.

4 weeks   4 weeks   4 weeks

Table 49. Frequency distribution (four-week schedule).

Number of Exposures	Percent Reach		Reach Difference
	Continuous Schedule	Flighted Schedule	
1 or more	91	95	4
2 or more	78	86	8
3 or more	64	76	12
4 or more	50	66	16
5 or more	38	56	18
6 or more	28	47	19
7 or more	20	39	19
8 or more	14	31	17
9 or more	10	25	15
10 or more	6	20	14
Schedule:	100 GRPs/week	150 GRPs/week	

four exposures, for example, then the flighted schedule has a distinct advantage in the short run.

Although much research has been conducted to answer the question of how much frequency is required to communicate the advertising message effectively, no one study has provided a definitive answer. The hypotheses of all these studies are:

- There is a direct relationship between frequency of exposure during a given period of time and advertising effectiveness.
- There is a minimum rate of exposure (frequency) below which the sales motivation value is either unproductive or marginal.
- There is a ceiling of frequency above which additional exposure is either unproductive or produces diminishing returns.
- There is decay in recall levels and established attitudes during hiatuses.
- Advertising effectiveness does *not* immediately cease when advertising is discontinued.

The dimensions of these factors may vary in accordance with the product's purchase cycle, stage of product development, product category, competitive environment, creative execution, media selection and media weights. If the media planner believes the hypotheses to be correct, and gives consideration to all these factors, then he or she establishes an effective frequency level against which to analyze both flighted and continuous scheduling patterns.

There are a number of alternative methods for scheduling media that can produce the effect of both flighting and continuous advertising simultaneously. For example, if the media plan is composed of two television dayparts, or national and local media, or two different media forms, each of the components can be flighted in an alternating pattern. Additionally, different broadcast stations, or different magazines, can be scheduled at different times producing a flighted effect for specific vehicles, and a continuous effect across the media form. (See Exhibit 23.)

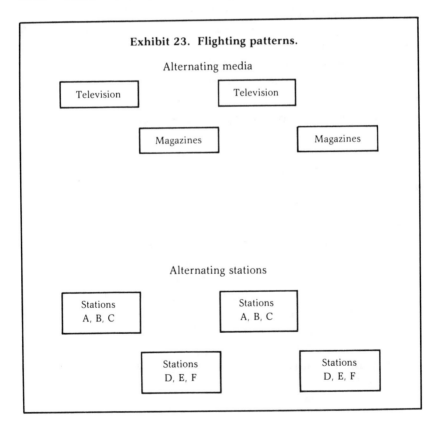

Exhibit 23. Flighting patterns.

Alternating media

| Television | Television |

| Magazines | Magazines |

Alternating stations

| Stations A, B, C | Stations A, B, C |

| Stations D, E, F | Stations D, E, F |

The media planner should bear in mind that even continuous advertising is received by the consumer in a flighted pattern. A schedule of one announcement per week in network television, for example, will be seen by some people only once, some people only twice, etc. The period between exposures to your advertising is indeed a hiatus in the consumer's perception. The technique of flighting advertising produces higher levels of activity during certain periods of time. This higher level of activity, in turn, generates higher levels of frequency of exposure and thereby shortens the hiatus period between exposures.

4. Coupon Objective

The media plan might require coupons be distributed via consumer media. The extent of distribution (number of coupons and geography) is outlined in the objective.

It is now the media planner's role to select the specific media to carry the coupons.

In addition to typical media considerations, factors of primary importance in evaluating media vehicles for coupon promotions include:

- The coupon form to be used and the availability of that form in media.
- Circulation distribution requirements—how many coupons are to be distributed.
- The distribution method of the media vehicle.
- Advertising space and redemption costs.
- Duplication among media vehicles.

There are several coupon forms and several media types that carry coupons. An insert coupon can be carried in magazines as a pop-up card, usually requiring the purchase of back-up page on which the card will lie. Inserts can also be distributed via direct mail, either as a co-op effort with other advertisers or as a solo venture. Most advertisers do not do solo couponing via direct mail as list generation and mailing costs are too high. Sharing these basic costs in a co-op mailing reduces the distribution cost substantially with only a slight reduction in redemption rate.

Many newspapers and supplements also make available free-standing inserts—pre-printed material not physically attached to the publication, but carried within the pages, or between sections. On-page coupons can be purchased in magazines, newspapers or supplements, with any cost premium over the usual rate for space. Stick-on coupons can be purchased in supplements. The edge of the card coupon is glued to the page.

Coupon redemption rates vary by type of coupon and by medium. Table 50 shows the average redemption rates for wide variety of coupon types as tabulated by A. C. Nielsen.

Table 50. Coupon redemption rates.	
Newspaper on-page	2.8%
Newspaper co-op	3.0
Magazine on-page	2.4
Magazine pop-up	5.1
Sunday Supplement—free-standing insert	4.3
Sunday Supplement on-page	2.4
Direct mail	8.0

If there is a marketing objective for total redemption, the media planner can estimate the number of coupons that will be redeemed by using the above redemption rates for each medium considered. This redemption data can also be used in combination with the media selection data (discussed later) to determine the cost-per-thousand of coupons redeemed by medium.

Magazines will generally limit the number of coupons accepted to one per signature (consists of 16–24 folded pages bound together to form a section). Some publications restrict the face value of a single coupon to the cost of their cover price, while some place a limit on the total cumulative value of insert coupons within a single issue. Both these restrictions are an attempt to reduce misredemption. When a magazine insert coupon which is redeemable at the store is involved, circulation is generally limited to subscription copies, to deter possible misredemption at the newsstand or distribution level.

For promotional use, media *circulation* values often override total audience measurements since passalong audiences may not have an equal opportunity to receive the offer because of its previous extraction by the primary reader. Additionally, one should give consideration to the value of an advertising page to the secondary reader if that page has been mutilated because the primary reader has cut out the coupon.

Therefore, media *coverage* should be analyzed on the basis of the number of copies distributed, rather than total audience only. Of primary importance is duplication among media vehicles. That combination of vehicles with the *least* duplication is most desirable as it will extend reach of the program to as many different prospects as possible and limit the delivery of more than one coupon to the same person.

The total cost of a coupon promotion is composed of the cost of advertising space and the absolute coupon redemption. Thus the type of coupon selected and the rate of redemption that can be expected from each media vehicle are important considerations when evaluting media alternatives.

5. Reach/Frequency Objective

Assume an objective has been established to maximize reach of women with a minimum of four advertising exposures per month (once per week). For demonstration ease, let us assume that network television has been chosen as the only medium to be used. The planner is now faced with deciding between network TV dayparts, and if a combination of dayparts are to be used, what proportions of each should be used.

The planner could start the analysis by devising as many alternative schedules as are affordable within the given budget. Shown in Table 51 are six alternatives (though the number of alternatives is nearly infinite).

The six levels are different in many ways. They produce different numbers of announcements, different women GRP levels, different cost efficiencies and different total women reach and average frequency. The only thing in common among the plans is that they are all national in scope (network television), and each costs the same amount of money ($1 million).

Table 51. Alternative media plan considerations.

Percent of $1,000,000 Budget

Plan	Primetime	Daytime	Late Evening	Early News
A	100	—	—	—
B	—	100	—	—
C	—	—	100	—
D	—	—	—	100
E	50	50	—	—
F	50	—	50	—

Table 52. Media plan comparison.

Plan	Number of :30 Announcements	Total Women GRPs	CPM	Total Women Reach/Frequency
A	10	120	$9.41	71/1.7
B	66	330	3.39	61/5.4
C	50	150	7.52	33/4.6
D	20	160	7.05	50/3.2
E	38	225	5.02	68/3.3
F	30	135	8.36	57/2.4

None of the above information, however, is useful in making a decision if the objective is *effective* reach (maximize reach of women with a minimum of four advertising exposures per month). The number of announcements is a function of the budget and the cost per commercial unit—it does not reveal anything about reach. Total women GRPs is informational and offers an indication of the gross delivery, but also does not reveal facts about reach. Cost-per-thousand is useful for assessing the efficiency of one alternative versus another, but again, no information about reach. Total women reach/ frequency, at first blush, might be used as the criterion for selecting one plan over another, but *average* frequency does not indicate the percentage of women who will be exposed to at least four advertising messages.

The planner must take the analysis a step further by calcu-lating a frequency distribution for each plan. The following table, based on a frequency distribution of each plan, exhibits the percentage of women who will be exposed to at least four advertising messages.

Plan	Women Reach at 4.0+ Frequency Level
A	2
B	32
C	15
D	17
E	24
F	12

Table 53. Effective reach comparisons.

Based on the above, the planner would opt for Plan B, composed of all daytime TV. This plan reaches more women who will be exposed to at least four advertising messages. If the planner had not done a frequency distribution, he or she might choose either Plan A because it generates more total reach than the other plans or Plan E because it produces the best balance of reach and frequency.

Although this analysis seems very straightforward, it is seldom that the planner has the flexibility to select media vehicles on the basis of accomplishing only one objective. Additionally, all analyses are complicated by a number of other factors which have an effect on how the planner addresses each medium at any point in time.

Costs, for example, fluctuate among network TV dayparts throughout the year based on supply and demand. Hypothetically, primetime network might be less cost efficient than late night network in one calendar quarter, and more cost efficient in another. The lower the cost-per-thousand, the more GRPs that can be purchased within a set budget. The more GRPs that can be purchased, the higher the reach and/or frequency that can be produced.

Let us take the above exercise one step further and assume that "communication values" are part of the media analysis. If we assume, for example, that daytime's communication value is 75 percent that of primetime, we could make a totally different strategy decision based on an analysis of effective reach. If primetime GRPs are valued at 100 percent, and daytime GRPs at 75 percent, then the effective GRPs for Plan E are 124 (as opposed to 225 when each daypart is given full value).

	Women GRPs	×	Value	=	Weighted Women GRPs
Primetime	60		100%		30
Daytime	125		75%		94
Total	225				124

Table 54. Weighting media by communications values.

If the planner calculates a frequency distribution based on the above weighted GRPs, the reach of women at the 4 + frequency level is 14. This is approximately the same effective reach as generated by Plan D (all early evening news). If an evaluation of effective reach does not reveal major differences among plan alternatives, or if other objectives bear importantly on media usage, then the planner must use other criteria to decide which media are most appropriate for accomplishing the objectives of the plan.

6. Testing Objective

Every media plan should have an objective to test advertising. Media/marketing tests are conducted to gain knowledge so better decisions can be made in the future. All tests have two things in common:

- They minimize the risk of incorrectly spending media funds.
- They are learning experiences from which we can extrapolate results for further use.

The most common test is of a complete marketing/media program developed for a new product prior to its national launch. Additionally, there are a number of other tests which can be conducted, all of which can provide useful information:

- **Spending levels.** A test of increased or decreased spending compared to the current level.
- **Allocation philosophy.** Spending where the business is versus where the business is not.
- **Scheduling.** Testing the effects of continuous advertising versus flighting.
- **Media mix.** Using different media than currently used, either exclusively or in combination with current media.
- **Copy length.** Using :30s versus :60s, or full pages versus half pages, etc.

Regardless of the test conducted, it is important to construct the test plan for the geographic area in which the plan would be implemented if the test is successful. For a new product planned for a national launch, the test must be national in scope. For a regionally distributed product (e.g., beer marketed only east of the Mississippi), the test plan must include all states in that region.

It is important that the national plan be translated down to the test market(s) rather than vice versa. In this manner, one is able to construct a plan that has national implication. If a plan is devised for the test market only, it might not be projectable to the universe, nor be affordable or implementable on a national basis.

Test markets should be representative of the universe to which results will be projected. If a national media plan is tested in markets which do not represent the U.S. in terms of sales, competitive activity, socio-economic factors, media consumption patterns, etc., results from the test might not be representative of what could happen in the U.S. as a whole.

Control markets should also be selected to read the effects of the current plan compared to the effects in the test markets where the media usage has been altered. Control markets should be selected on the same basis as test markets and therefore be carefully matched to the test markets. Both control and test markets should have adequate auditing facilities and/or sales data in order to make proper comparisons.

The national plan should be constructed for the period in which it will run (assuming the test results are positive) rather than for the period in which it will be tested. If a national plan is constructed for calendar year 1986, and tested in 1986, it might not be affordable in 1987 due to constantly increasing costs for all media.

Once test markets are selected there is a choice between two testing methods:

> **1. Little U.S. Method.** This simulates in test market the advertising *pressure* which is generated by the national media plan in the *average* U.S. market.

This test philosophy assumes the test area is truly representative of the total U.S. and that results occurring in this area are representative of what will happen nationally.

The example shows a national media plan composed of network TV, magazines and spot TV in markets which represent 60 percent of U.S. households.

Table 55. Alternative testing procedures (total women GRPs).

	National Plan	Test Market Little U.S.	Test Market As It Falls
Network TV	400	400	380
Magazines	100	100	120
Spot TV (60% U.S.)			
A Markets	150	—	—
B Markets	100	—	100
C Markets	50	—	—
Average	100	60	—
Total		560	600

To translate the national plan into test market, the *average* activity is scheduled. For both national media (network TV and magazines), the test market receives the average of the national weight. For spot TV, the test market receives the average of markets receiving spot TV and not receiving spot TV (100 GRPs in 60 percent of the U.S. plus zero GRPs in 40 percent of the U.S. for a weighted total of 60 GRPs).

2. As It Falls Method. In this method, the test markets receive the advertising pressure they normally would receive under the national plan.

Underlying this method is the premise that all products have variations in sales potential and test markets should recognize these differences.

With a "Little U.S." method in the example shown, the test market receives 560 GRPs, simulating the *average* weight delivered in the *average* market. In fact, no market in the U.S. might actually receive this level within the National Plan. With the "As It Falls" method, GRP activity varies according to the local delivery of national media forms, and according to the delivery of the local media forms being used.

Both methods can be used to project test results to the U.S. Regardless of which method is employed, most research professionals would advise that more than one test market be used. Ideally, several markets should be included in the test which collectively represent the true average of the national media plan.

Within either testing method it is desirable to schedule local activity that closely resembles the national media being used. Following are the guidelines for local media use:

- **Television.** Use cut-ins whenever possible for network TV. A *cut-in* is the placement of the test commercial in the test market within the network program. The nationally scheduled commercial is cut-over (replaced) by the test commercial. This technique requires you to have network TV scheduled for the test period. With this method, the viewer in the test market sees what she or he normally would see if the test plan were implemented nationally.

  If cut-ins are not available, spot TV can be used to simulate the network TV weight. However, there are differences between spot TV and network TV in terms of audience composition, program type, in-program announcements in network versus some spot announcements being aired between programs and reach/frequency accumulation. It is therefore general practice to compensate for the differences by

Table 56. Local media simulation of national plan delivery.

National Plan	Test Market
Night network TV	1. Cut-ins 2. Prime spot (plus compensation) 3. Fringe spot (plus compensation) 4. Cable TV
Day network TV	1. Cut-ins 2. Day spot (plus compensation) 3. Cable TV
Spot TV	1. Spot TV 2. Cable TV
Network radio	Spot radio
Spot radio	Spot radio
Magazines	1. Test market editions 2. Other magazines 3. Supplements 4. Newspapers
Newspapers/supplements	Newspapers/supplements
Outdoor/transit	Outdoor/transit

purchasing more GRPs in spot TV than would normally be scheduled via network TV.

- **Radio.** Unlike the differences between network TV and spot TV, network radio and spot radio are virtually identical in terms of environment, commercial positioning and reach/frequency accumulation. Therefore, network radio can be directly translated into spot radio. Further, there are no adjustments necessary for translating spot radio in the national plan to spot radio in the test market.

- **Print.** If local editions of the magazines used in the national plan are not available in the selected test markets, other magazines with similar editorial formats should be used. If magazines are not available in the test markets, newspaper supplements can be used as the first alternative, and newspapers as the second alternative.

Although neither supplements nor newspapers have the same editorial environment or readership pattern as magazines, it is best to use these media rather than using totally unrelated media, or not using any print media at all. It is important, however, to analyze the delivery of the local print vehicles relative to the national print media to ensure that there are not wide variations in coverage.

- **Outdoor/Transit.** As both are local media forms, both can be translated directly.

How Much to Spend
on Advertising

There is never a clearcut amount of money that should be appropriated from the marketing budget to mount a successful advertising campaign. With the exception of experimental formulas, there are no quick and dirty methods that we can use to define the optimum amount of money to be invested in advertising media. And even if there were magic answers, there are innumerable outside factors that influence the appropriation—from the profit margin of the brand, to the financial stability of the corporation, to competitive pressures, to the cost of media and advertising production.

The question of how much to spend requires detailed analysis on the part of the advertiser and the advertising agency to assess sales potential and affordability. The media planner's role in this decision-making process is limited. The planner can accumulate competitive advertising expenditures and guide the advertiser as to the cost of media and the audience delivery affordable at given budget levels.

How much to spend on advertising is a strategic decision. The advertising budget must be viewed as a function of the marketing and selling objectives of the brand or company. To have ambitious marketing goals supported by modest advertising budgets is irreconcilable. Conversely, it makes no financial sense to have an ambitious budget if the marketing goals are modest.

The role of advertising must be clearly defined, and its task must be decided before determining how much should be spent. Until the advertising task has been determined, you cannot apply the necessary discipline and available techniques to calculate how much money is required.

Factors to consider before choosing a spending technique include:

1. The market in which your brand (or service) will compete.

   The competitive environment must be selected to determine how much money you will need to accomplish your goals. For example, if you are advertising lemonade, you might decide to compete against all other lemonades, or all non-carbonated beverages, or all citrus beverages, or all refreshment beverages including soft drinks. The amount of advertising money being spent in each of these categories varies dramatically. Therefore, spending for your brand could represent a major or minor portion of the total category.

   Inherent in the competitive decision is the choice of demographic target. If you are going to compete only against other lemonades, for example, you might select an adult target, versus targeting adults, teens and children if you choose to compete against all refreshment beverages. The more expansive the demographic target, the more money will be required to reach all consumer segments.

2. Where you will advertise.

   Invariably, all brands have pockets of strengths and weaknesses across the country. Spending decisions must take these variations into consideration. The same rate of spending in every city or region will not necessarily produce the same results because of the competitive environment variations from city to city and other environment and media cost factors.

   It is not sufficient simply to know the amount of sales in each city or region. You must determine the share of market in each location and the reason that share exists. For example, poor sales in a particular area could be the result of distribution deficiencies, pricing policies, sales force weaknesses, or the strength of a specific local brand. Knowing the reasons will help you judge the contribution that might, or might not, be made by advertising. This, in turn, can guide you in spending policies.

3. The ability of advertising to effect a sales change or accomplish a specific goal.

    Depending on the objective to be achieved, the condition of the brand (or service) to be advertised and the marketing environment as a whole, a decision could be made *not* to advertise. Advertising cannot be a panacea for all deficiencies. For example, if a product distribution deficiency exists whereby the product cannot reach the consumer, or is sold in inadequate quantities, any dollar spent in advertising would be wasted. If the product itself is inadequate and cannot match the competition, advertising might promote first-time trials among consumers but probably would not convince consumers to purchase the product again.

Once these factors are considered, and a decision is made to advertise, there are a number of different techniques that can be used to determine how much to spend and how to allocate those dollars. Four methods are discussed here.

- **Advertising/Sales Ratio Method.** This is the most popularly used method for determining advertising budgets. Advertising expenditures are considered an integral part of the marketing budget of a product and funds are set aside as a *cost of doing business*. The ratio used will vary widely among corporations, and often among different products within a corporation. For packaged goods, the advertising budget can also be expressed in terms of *case rate*—the amount of money to be spent for each case of product sold.

    While the appropriation for advertising is part of the marketing budget, it is nevertheless the most vulnerable cost element. Manufacturing and distribution costs, as well as profit margins, are usually fixed. The only flexible marketing cost is the amount of money to be spent in advertising. Therefore, while budgets could be derived using the Advertising/Sales Ratio Method, they are quite often subject to revision.

There are strengths and weaknesses in the A/S approach. The strengths are:

—it is self-correcting in regard to sales performance and maintains a consistent profit margin for the brand.

—it is relatively easy to manage the budget allocation.

—the relationship is easily understood and generally suits the interests of both the financial and marketing groups.

—an implicit incentive system operates whereby increased sales generate additional funds to support an aggressive advertising program, while the brand is penalized for poor sales.

The weaknesses of the A/S system are:

—the requirements for an advertising program do not always follow directly with sales, particularly when brand sales are declining and increased advertising may not be the cure.

—considerable historical information is required to determine the correct A/S ratio.

—variable A/S ratios should be used by area, which requires exhaustive analysis.

—the basic assumption of a direct linear relationship between advertising and sales might not be true.

• **Share of Advertising.** In this system the advertising budget is chosen as a *share of total category advertising spending*. In the vernacular, it is sometimes called the *share of noise*, where noise refers to the total advertising to which consumers are exposed.

As with the A/S method, there are strengths and weaknesses in this system. The strengths are:

—it positions your advertising budget competitively.

—you can react to competitive changes in advertising such as new brands entering the market.

—it places expectations for the advertising effort in a realistic perspective. For example, if you spend half as much as your nearest competitor, you cannot expect to exceed that competitor's share of market.

The weaknesses are:

—the information you gather might not be accurate since competitive advertising expenditure data is not easily obtained.

—the basic assumption of a direct relationship between share of advertising and share of market might not be true.

—unless the right competitive market is defined, the wrong budget will be calculated.

—share of *advertising* might be too narrow a view when one considers the influences of point-of-sale material, promotions, etc.

—competitors could be dictating your budget and lead you into spending at the wrong rate.

• **Mathematical Models.** There are a number of formulas that have been developed to determine how much to spend. One formula, developed by the Hendry Corporation, for example, describes the interrelationships between advertising, share of market and profits. From this, Hendry is able to determine how much money should be spent in advertising to maximize profits, and how much could be spent in advertising to maximize share of market.

The basic strength of using a mathematical model is that it usually includes *all* factors that influence customers' purchasing decisions—advertising, promotion, pricing, competitive environment, etc.

The weakness of using such a model is that you must spend time and money to find out if it works. It is impossible to determine if any model works without "real world" experience in the marketplace to determine if X budget produces Y result.

• **Task Method.** Here is where the media planner can play a significant part in the decision. This method requires the establishment of actionable marketing and media objectives and the writing of an advertising plan to achieve the task at hand.

As previously discussed, media objectives require extensive investigation and thought. However, once specific objectives are set forth, we can use simple mathematical procedures to determine the cost of purchasing media to accomplish these objectives. The objectives can be media-related (such as providing a certain level of reach and frequency over a given period of time); marketing related (such as the need to generate a certain amount of trial of a new product); or any combination of these.

The strength and weakness of this system are interrelated. If we know precisely what advertising levels are required to accomplish a task, the system is very powerful. However, if we do not know (and this is usually the case), this approach is highly subjective and therefore questionable.

Lastly, a task method approach does not concern itself with a brand's profitability. The amount of money required under this method may not bear any relation to what is affordable.

How to Present Media

The objectives of the media presentation are to:

- Display clearly the direction of the media plan.
- Inform the client of the key ingredients.
- Convince the client that the media plan is the best solution to the marketing problem.

The presentation can take one of four visual forms and the one used depends on the size of audience, the amount of material to be presented and the complexity of the material shown. The decision to use one of these forms should be made well in advance of the final preparation of material to ensure that the correct typeface is used and that the amount of material on a given page or chart befits the presentation form.

Through-the-Book. This form of presentation is generally used in smaller, informal meetings. The planner literally walks the client through the media plan, page by page, reading the contents and highlighting the more important aspects. With this form of presentation, the planner can present very complex information and allow the audience to spend as much time as desired on each page. Control is therefore more difficult than with other forms where the planner totally controls the pace of the presentation. It is very important that each page be numbered and that the planner periodically remind the audience which page is being discussed. If you don't do this, you lose the audience—everybody will be on different pages, some well ahead of where you want them to be.

Blow-up Charts. This form is more formal than the through-the-book form, but it also is for use only in smaller meetings. The physical size of the charts is generally not large enough to be seen by people sitting more than 10 feet away. The material presented should be less cluttered than with the through-the book method: Tighter sentences (but never cryptic); more use of bar charts and graphs than actual numbers; less detail.

Transparencies. The use of transparencies with an overhead projector is a compromise between the previous two forms of presentations. It allows you to present more detailed material to a larger audience, but it lacks the visual quality of blow-up charts.

Slides. This is the most formal of the presentation forms and can be used for any size audience. It is also the highest quality form and the most expensive to produce. Media plans are usually not presented in this fashion except on certain occasions, such as a presentation to very large audiences, new business presentations, etc.

In presenting media, bear in mind that much of the language is complex and at least one person in the room generally will not be familiar with the jargon of GRPs, reach, frequency, etc. The planner should address this by offering a brief explanation of the terms as they are used.

Presenting the numbers on a chart is sometimes more difficult than constructing the chart. The audiences should be walked through all the numbers carefully so they have full appreciation of what is being presented. A good way to present numerical data is to approach it step by step, reading from left to right, from top to bottom:

Table 57. Profile of adult women who drink carbonated soft drinks.

	% Pop.	Drank any in last month		Drank low-calorie cola in last month	
		%	Index	%	Index
Total women	100.0	83.0	100	17.6	100
18–24	17.9	94.4	170	22.1	126
25–34	20.7	90.0	99	21.7	123
35–44	15.5	86.3	85	18.8	107
45–54	15.6	83.4	84	19.9	113
55–64	13.7	78.5	86	12.2	69
65 & older	17.1	63.2	76	9.7	55

Source: W. R. Simmons

1. Describe the purpose of the chart: This chart shows carbonated soft drink consumption by women by age.
2. Read the column headings across: We display the distribution of population by age, the percentage of each age group who drank soft drinks in the last month and the percentage of each age group who drank low-calorie cola-type soft drinks in that period.
3. Read the first vertical column: We show this data for each age group: Total women, women aged 18 to 24, 25 to 34, 35 to 44, etc.
4. Read the numerical data vertically: Women aged 18 to 24 represent 17.9 percent of all adult women; women 25 to 34 account for 20.7 percent of the total women population, etc.
5. Read the next column of data, relating it to the first, from top to bottom: Of all adult women, 83 percent drank a soft drink in the last month; 94.4 percent of women aged 18 to 24 drank soft drinks in the last month, and as we move into older age groups, the percentage who drank soft drinks declines.
6. Explain mathematical computations, if any: If we divide the 94.4 percent women in the 18 to 24 age group by the average consumption for all women of 83 percent, we arrive at an index of 170, indicating that the concentration of soft drink drinkers is 70 percent greater among 18- to 24-year-olds than that found in the population as a whole. Note that the index drops as we move through the age groups, showing that as a woman gets older, she is increasingly less likely to be a soft drink consumer.
7. Explain additional material: We have also displayed the percentage of women who drank low-calorie cola-type soft drinks to see if they have a different profile. They do. Note that the index is above 100 for women in the four age groups from 18 to 54, indicating that the low-calorie drinker tends to be slightly older in profile than the average soft drink consumer.

Regardless of the data you present, or the makeup of the audience, it is imperative that you be totally familiar with the material and that you have rehearsed, rehearsed, rehearsed.

Generally, the media planner should present the media plan to the client. Aside from pride of authorship, the planner is the expert, knowing more about media than anyone else in the room. The intricacies of the construction, as well as intimate knowledge of the components, argue that the planner should make the presentation, both to explain and to field any questions/problems that might arise at the presentation.

Notwithstanding the above, keep in mind that the objectives of the presentation are to inform, convince, and get approval. If for any reason the planner or buyer cannot present, the presentation should nevertheless go forth.

Media Creativity

The function of the media planner is to *effectively* and *efficiently* bring together the message and the right audience. While the planner should consider himself or herself a money manager looking for the greatest return on investment, he or she should not overlook that creative uses of media oftentimes provide a level of impact and effectiveness which transcend normal cost efficiencies. Utilizing all the resources for proper media planning will lead to the most logical and sound solutions, but not necessarily the *best* plan.

Effectiveness of the media program, and not necessarily efficiency, is a key criterion in the development and execution of a media program. Cost per results instead of cost-per-thousand must be the watchword.

The media function does not exist in a vacuum. It must be planned and implemented as an extension of marketing and creative needs. Every media action must have a marketing rationale. The media planner has an obligation to be creative, just as much as do other areas of an advertising agency.

Following are miscellaneous examples of creative uses of media:

American Express — When American Express wanted to develop the use of credit cards for purchasing theater tickets, the company bought time in the Tony Awards on television. Peter Ustinov was the spokesman in a 30-second commercial that was set on a stage and podium quite similar to that used in the program. Viewers did not see Ustinov as a commercial, but rather as a continuation of the TV show.

No-Doz—This stay-awake pill with a small advertising budget and a small target market purchased the seldom-used environment of late night radio—the right medium for an appropriately timed message to reach tired drivers.

Old Crow—The advertising theme for this best-selling bourbon was tied to historical moments in sports. Positioning for every magazine advertisement was negotiated to run opposite any sports editorial feature. The upshot—more involvement with the reader.

Contac—Positioned for hay fever sufferers, Contac timed its advertising to air in selected markets when the pollen count started to rise. Commercials were scheduled in radio weathercasts immediately after the pollen count for the day was announced. Hay fever sufferers were attuned to the message.

Max-Pax—Looking for frequency but not in a position to triple advertising expenditures, the brand scheduled special one-third page units in magazines. Three separate advertisements were scheduled in each issue, and each one-third page was the only advertisement on the page—page dominance, reader involvement and frequency for little more than the cost of single full-page ads.

Pepperidge Farm—This baker produces a variety of cakes and pastries. But each item had a small budget. Digest-size island units were placed opposite each other in magazines giving each product advertising impact and at the same time establishing a *line identity* for Pepperidge Farm.

Burger Chef—To reach adults *and* children, newspaper comics were selected, but with unique usage. The french fry bag used at Burger Chef was glued onto the page and invited readers to visit a store to have the bag filled.

Ban—Soon after this deodorant was introduced, it was faced with overpowering competitive pressures. Ban's advertising pressure was increased in television four-fold without any increase in budget. Instead of using 60-second TV commercials, special 15-minute commercials were produced and tagged onto companion 45-second commercials.

Open Pit—Open Pit was positioned as a barbecue sauce during the short summer selling season. Ten-second identification commercials were aired in primetime television for quick reach and heavy frequency. To extend the media concept into the winter, when the brand was positioned as a cooking ingredient, small space newspaper advertisements were purchased, each ad looking like a recipe card.

Shell—During the controversial oil crisis period, Shell needed to keep its name prominent, without demonstrating product. The idea was very big, but the commercial used was very small. Shell sponsored CBS' "Bicentennial Minute" over a two-year period having only a five-second identification at the end of the program. Viewers perceived the entire minute as a Shell commercial.

Principles of Media Management

Numbers don't think . . . people do.

In his "Magic Lantern," David Ogilvy said: "Look before you leap." Sound research and thorough investigation, combined with intelligence and logic, are mandatory before astute media decisions can be made. But too often these decisions are based on *numbers alone.*

Numbers are a big part of the media planner's and media buyer's life. They are used to analyze alternatives, provide direction and eventually help make a decision. Too often, however, the numbers are used as a crutch—as the primary rationale for selecting one medium over another or one television spot rather than another. They are often viewed myopically. All that goes into generating the numbers, all the varying research techniques used, and all the pitfalls and dangers surrounding the numbers, are blurred.

The computer has been a windfall, almost a necessity. A myriad of numbers can be fed in and the computer can be programmed to spit out an equally mind-boggling list; a list fashioned to any number of needs and displayed with clarity in order to allow one to simply run one's fingers down the columns to choose the best answer. The advances in sophisticated decisions in a more competitive climate, in turn, argue for use of the computer to deal with the multiple machinations.

Media planning is now a sophisticated art managed along scientific principles. It is an integral part of the advertising agency and a primary aspect of every marketing plan. There are now more media outlets than ever, with more complicated research to prove one superior to the other. Costs for media

This chapter originally was published as a Features column in *Advertising Age*, May 21, 1979.

are skyrocketing, making investment decisions even more critical. The broadcast marketplace is extremely volatile causing buyers to constantly monitor pricing and programming. No easy task.

Something could easily get lost. Sometimes the quantity of numbers generated prevents planners and buyers from spending the time to look into the numbers and see what made them happen in the first place. Sometimes the numbers become the rationale rather than the guideline. Sometimes the human element is lost and creative thinking is subjugated to an almost nonexistent role. And that is a pity.

What should we media planners do? Here are ten guidelines:

1. Be a money manager.

The client has entrusted you with his or her money to make the *best* media decisions. Your recommendations become an investment—and the client is looking for the greatest return-on-investment. Never forget that the numbers in a media plan are backed with *real* dollars.

2. Remember effectiveness is primary.

Effectiveness, and not necessarily efficiency, is the key criterion. Go beyond the numbers in making recommendations that will deliver more effective advertising. Have the guts to defend your opinions. Appreciate that all the numbers are *estimates*, based on a sampling of the population. They can swing up or down depending on the research technique, the time of year and the particular sample chosen. All the numbers have statistical tolerance, a leeway for variation that can be expected from the average number shown. Decisions based on a ten-cent difference in a cost-per-thousand, or a two percent advantage of one plan over another, are shaky. In the real world, the exact opposite might be true.

3. Be creative.

Andrew Kershaw said: "A copywriter is called creative, but is not the only person in the agency who is creative." The creative idea can be big and expensive, but more often it is little more than a better way of doing the usual. Think. Innovate. Create.

4. Be conversant with all media forms.

Specializing in one medium, to the exclusion of all others, breeds narrow thinking. Read all trade journals and textbooks available. Attend seminars, speeches and conventions related to media. Rub elbows with fellow planners and buyers, and media salespeople, to keep on top of the latest developments. You'll become more rounded in your profession and thereby make a more significant contribution.

5. Evaluate all reasonable alternatives.

This is hard work, and it takes time. But to make hasty recommendations for the sake of expedience can result in a lackluster, ineffective plan and execution. Use the computer's capabilities.

6. Be involved in the total marketing picture.

A media plan is an extension of the marketing plan and should reflect the marketing objectives and creative strategy. Media planning and buying cannot exist in a vacuum and be effective. Involvement with the account and creative groups, as well as with the client and his product, is mandatory.

7. Maintain what you have built.

Maintenance is as important as building. The media plan that is executed does not always perform as anticipated. Significant losses in delivery and effectiveness can result if a television spot is missed or reproduction in a magazine is poor. Take the time to monitor performance. Upgrade when possible and correct discrepancies immediately.

8. Keep everyone informed.

You are the expert in media and charged with devising and executing media plans with sound rationale. Your job becomes easier and more productive if the account groups, creative groups, the client and your fellow media colleagues know what is happening in the total media scene. Dissemination of information argues for a discipline of thinking and begets better media recommendations. Shower your clients with information.

9. Establish rapport with media suppliers.

Media salespeople often know more about their specific medium than you do. They can be a storehouse of pertinent information that will help your media decisions. Let them into your office, return their phone calls. Be candid in your dealings with them and let them know your needs in order to have fruitful meetings that can benefit the client in the long run.

10. Contribute beyond media.

You are an advertising person who happens to be expert in media. Your greatest contribution to the client will be in your specialty, but this should not inhibit you from recommending marketing, creative or new product ideas that can build the client's business.

Glossary/Index

Area of Dominant Influence (ADI)—See **TV Market.**

Adjacency—A program or time period that is scheduled immediately preceding or following a scheduled program on the same station. Also called **Break Position** (p. 86).

Affiliate—A broadcast station bound to a contractual relationship with one or more networks to carry network originated programs and announcements (p. 85).

Agate Line—A newspaper space measurement that measures one column wide and 1/14" deep.

AM (Amplitude Modulation)—The transmission of sound in radio broadcasting in which the amplitude (power) of a transmitting wave is modulated (changed) to simulate the original sound. There are currently about 4,500 AM radio stations in the U.S.

Announcement—An advertising message in broadcast media. Announcements generally are of :60, :30, :20 or :10 duration. Synonymous with "commercial."

As It Falls—A method for simulating media plans in test markets (p. 136).

Audience Composition—The demographic profile of audiences of a particular advertising medium (p. 63).

Audimeter—An electronic device attached to TV sets in sample households of A. C. Nielsen. It records set usage and channel tuned on a minute-by-minute basis.

Audit Bureau of Circulations (A.B.C.)—An organization formed by media, advertisers and advertising agencies to audit the circulation statements of its member magazines and newspapers.

Availability—The commercial position in a program or between programs on a given station or network that is available for purchase by an advertiser. "Avails" for short.

Average Audience—In broadcast, the number of homes (or individuals) tuned to the average minute of a program. In print media, the number of individuals who looked into an average issue of a publication.

Barter—The acquisition of quantities of commercial time from broadcast stations in exchange for merchandise.

Billboard—In broadcast, free air-time given to a sponsoring advertiser (p. 87). In outdoor media, an advertising structure (p. 91).

Black & White Page—An advertising page that uses no color. Abbreviated as P B/W.

Bleed—In print media, to extend the illustration or copy to the edge of a page so there is no white border. In outdoor, a poster panel which uses the entire available space.

Brand Development Index (BDI)—A numerical display indicating the geographic or demographic areas of a product's strength or weakness (p. 57).

Break Position—A commercial aired between programs as opposed to within a program. Also called **Adjacency** (p. 86).

Broadcast Coverage Area—The geographic area within which a signal from an originating television station can be received (p. 65).

Busorama—An advertising unit within transit media (p. 93).

Cable TV (CATV)—Community Antenna TV provides special lines rented by a firm to a household either to bring in outside television stations, with a clear picture, and/or provide special programming on a direct hook-up.

Car Card—An advertising unit within transit media (p. 93).

Cash Discount—A discount granted by the media to an advertiser for prompt payment, usually amounting to 2 percent of the net amount.

Chain Break—The time between network programs when a network affiliated station identifies itself.

Circulation—In print media, the number of copies sold or distributed by a publication. In broadcast, the number of homes owning a set within a station's coverage area. In outdoor, the number of people passing an advertisement who have an opportunity to view it.

Clearance—The broadcast stations carrying a network program.

Clock Spectacular—An advertising unit within transit media (p. 93).

Closing Date—The date set by a publication for receipt of material for an advertisement to appear in a forthcoming issue.

Combination Rate—A special rate for advertisers using both morning and evening editions of a newspaper, or more than one vehicle in a group of publications.

Continuity Discount—A rate discount allowed an advertiser who purchases a specific schedule within a series of a publication's issues.

Controlled Circulation—The circulation of a publication that is sent free and addressed to specified individuals.

Cost-Per-Thousand—The cost per 1,000 individuals (or homes) delivered by a medium or media schedule (p. 59).

County Size—Designation of a county into one of four categories as defined by A. C. Nielsen based on population (p. 70).

Coupons—(p. 128).

Coverage—The percentage of persons (or homes) covered by a medium.

Cut-In—The insertion of a commercial, at the local level, into a network program (p. 136).

Day Parts—Times of broadcast for television and radio (p. 78).

Daytime—In TV, the daytime hours of programming, usually 10 a.m. to 4:30 p.m. EST (p. 78). In radio, generally 10:00 a.m. to 3:00 p.m. EST (p. 80).

Delayed Broadcast (DB)—The term given to a network TV program that is delayed for airing at a different time in a given market (p. 83).

Demographic Editions—Special editions of magazines directed to specific audience types (p. 90).

Designated Market Area (DMA)—See **TV Market.**

Drive Time—The morning and afternoon hours of radio broadcasting. Morning Drive: 6 to 10 a.m.; Afternoon Drive: 3 to 7 p.m. (p. 80).

Duplication—The number of individuals (or homes) exposed to more than one advertising message through a media schedule (p. 23, 37).

Effective Reach—The number of individuals (or homes) reached by a media schedule at a given level of frequency (p. 43).

Efficiency—The relationship of media cost to audience delivery. See **Cost-Per-Thousand.**

Exposure—A person's physical contact (visual and/or audio) with an advertising medium or message.

Fixed Position—In broadcast, a commercial unit purchased with non-preemption guarantees. In print, a position guaranteed to the advertiser in specified issues.

Flat Rate—The non-discountable rate charged by a newspaper for advertising.

Flighting—In broadcast, scheduling a heavy advertising effort for a period of time, followed by a hiatus, then coming back with another schedule at the same, higher, or lower level (p. 124).

Four-Color Page—An advertising page that utilizes three colors as well as black. Abbreviated as P 4-C or 4-C P.

Franchise Position—A valued position because of editorial adjacency, program value or geographical location.

Frequency—The number of times individuals (or homes) are exposed to an advertising message (p. 29).

Frequency Discount—A rate discount allowed an advertiser who purchases a specific schedule within a specified period of time.

Frequency Distribution—The array of reach according to the level of frequency delivered to each group (p. 41).

FM (Frequency Modulation)—A clear radio signal, without static or fading, that results from the adjustment of the frequency of the transmitting wave to the originating sound. There are currently about 3,800 FM stations in the U.S.

Fringe Time—In TV, the evening hours that precede and follow primetime, usually 4:30–7:30 p.m. and 11 p.m.–1 a.m. EST (p. 78).

Gatefold—A folded advertising page which, unfolded, is bigger in dimension than the regular page.

Gross Rating Points (GRPs)—The sum of ratings delivered by a given list of media vehicles (p. 17).

Hiatus—A period of non-activity.

Hi-Fi—Advertising on a continuous roll of paper that is fed into and becomes a preprinted insert in a newspaper. The completed advertisement, usually run on a heavier-than-newspaper stock and in full color, resembles a wallpaper pattern.

Homes Using TV (HUT)—The percentage of homes using TV at a given time (p. 7).

Identification (ID)—In broadcast, a commercial that is not over 10 seconds long (visual) and 8 seconds long (audio).

Impressions—The sum of all exposures (p. 19).

Independent Station—A broadcast station not affiliated with a line network (p. 84).

Index—A percentage which relates numbers to a base (p. 55).

In-Home Readers—Those people reading a magazine in their own home (p. 72).

Issue Life—The length of time it takes a magazine to be read by the maximum measurable audience (p. 75).

Junior Panel—A scaled-down version of a 24-sheet poster (p. 91).

Lead-In (Lead-Out)—Program preceding (or following) the time period or program being analyzed.

Line Networks—TV signals transmitted over telephone lines from one station to the next (p. 82).

Little U.S.—A method for simulating media plans in test markets (p. 135).

Magazine Audiences—(p. 72).

Makegood—In broadcast, a commercial position given in lieu of the announcement missed due to the fault of the station or network. In print, the free repeat of an advertisement to compensate for the publication's error in the original insertion.

Media Mix—(p. 24).

Merchandising—Promotional activities that complement advertising and which are provided free or at a nominal charge by media purchased for advertising.

Metro Area—Also **MSA** (p. 68).

Milline Rate—In newspapers, the cost per agate line per 1,000,000 circulation.

Network Broadcast Media—(p. 82).

Objectives, Media—The statement of action required of media to fulfill marketing needs (p. 103).

O & Os—The stations owned and operated by the three broadcast networks (p. 83).

Open Rate—The maximum rate charged by a magazine—its rate for one insertion.

Outdoor—(p. 91).

Out-of-Home Readers—Those people reading a magazine outside of their own homes (p. 72).

Painted Bulletin—An outdoor advertising structure on which advertising is painted directly (p. 92).

Participation—The purchase of an individual announcement within network TV; the purchase of an announcement in-program in spot TV (p. 86).

Passalong Readers—Readers of a publication which they or other members of their household did not purchase (p. 72).

Penetration—The proportion of persons (or homes) that are physically able to be exposed to a medium.

People Using Radio—The percentage of people using radio at a given time (p. 7).

People Using TV (PUT)—The percentage of people using TV at a given time (p. 7).

Point-of-Purchase Display—An advertising display at the place where consumers purchase goods or services (e.g., counter card at a retail outlet).

Porta-Panel—A mobile poster panel that is wheeled to a given location (e.g., a supermarket parking lot).

Poster Panel—An outdoor advertising structure on which a pre-printed advertisement is displayed (p. 91).

Preemption—The displacement of a regularly scheduled program, or announcement, on a broadcast facility by the station or network.

Primary Market Area—A geographic area defined by a newspaper (p. 69).

Primary Readers—Readers who purchased a magazine or are members in a household where the publication was purchased (p. 72).

Prime Access—The half-hour immediately preceding prime-time television in which local stations were originally charged by the Federal Communications Commission to broadcast programs in the interest of the local community (p. 78).

Primetime—In TV, a three-hour time period (Monday–Saturday) and three-and-a-half-hour time period (Sunday) designated by a station as its highest viewing time. Usually 8–11 p.m. (Monday–Saturday) and 7:30-11 p.m. (Sunday) EST (p. 78). In radio, generally 6–10 a.m. and 3–7 p.m. EST (p.80).

Psychographics—A term identifying personality characteristics and attitudes that affect a person's life style and purchasing behavior.

Pulsing—A flighting technique that calls for a continuous base of support augmented by intermittent bursts of heavy pressure (p. 124).

Quintile Distribution—A display of frequency among audiences grouped into equal fifths of total reach (p. 47).

Radio Daypart—(p. 80).

Radio Station Groups—(p. 85).

Rate Base—The circulation of a print vehicle upon which advertising space rates are based; it may or may not be guaranteed by the publication.

Rate Holder—A unit of space or time, usually small, that is used to maintain or establish a contractual agreement over a period of time.

Rating—The percentage of individuals (or homes) exposed to a particular TV or radio program (p. 4).

Reach—The number of different individuals (or homes) exposed to a media schedule within a given period of time (p. 21).

Readers Per Copy—The number of individuals reading a given issue of a publication (p. 75).

Rebate—A payment to the advertiser by a medium when the advertising schedule exceeds the contractual commitments originally agreed to and the advertisement earns a lower rate.

Retail Trading Zone—A geographic area around a central city (p. 70).

R.O.P.—Run-of-Press. A position request to run an advertisement anywhere in the publication.

Roll-Out—A marketing procedure where advertising is expanded into progressively more areas over time. See **Testing** (p. 133).

Rotary Display—The purchase of painted bulletins whereby the display face is periodically rotated to new locations (p. 92).

Scatter—Purchasing announcements in broadcast in many different programs.

Sets In Use—Antiquated and replaced by **Homes Using TV**. Referred to the number of sets turned on at a given time.

Share—The percentage of Homes Using TV (or radio) tuned to a particular program (p. 11).

Sheets—The number of pieces of paper needed to cover a poster panel area (p. 91).

Short Rate—In print media, the dollar penalty an advertiser pays for not fulfilling space requirements that were contracted for at the beginning of a given period, usually one year. The penalty is the difference in rate between the contracted rate and the actual earned rate.

Showing—Gross Rating Points within outdoor advertising (p. 91). The number of posters displayed on different vehicles within transit media (p. 93).

Simulcast—The concurrent broadcasting of a television or radio program.

SMSA—Standard Metropolitan Statistical Area (p. 68).

Special—Broadcast program that is not a part of the usual programming offered by a station or network.

Spectacolor—An advertising insert in newspapers, similar to Hi-Fi, but trimmed at the correct place.

Split Run—A scheduling technique whereby two different pieces of copy are run in the circulation of a publication with no one reader receiving both advertisements.

Sponsorship—The purchase of more than one announcement within a program allowing advertisers to receive bonus time via billboards (p. 86).

Spot TV or Radio—(p. 86).

Stategies, Media—The media solution used to fulfill the media objectives (p. 113).

Supplements—(p. 90).

Survey Area—See Total Survey Area.

Syndication—A method of placing a program on a market-by-market basis (p. 87).

Tabloid—A newspaper smaller than the size of standard newspaper, such as the *New York Daily News*.

Television Daypart—(p. 78).

Tolerance—The range of error, plus or minus the reported number, in audience research for any medium (p. 95).

Total Survey Area—In radio, the area in which radio signals from an originating market can be received (p. 67).

Transit—(p. 93).

TV Market—An unduplicated television area to which a county is assigned on the basis of highest share of viewing (p. 66).

UHF (Ultra High Frequency)—The band added to the VHF band for television transmission—channels 14–83.

VHF (Very High Frequency)—TV channels 2–13.

Viewers Per Set—The number of people viewing or listening to a program in each home.